The Return of Political Patronage

The Return of Political Patronage

How special advisers are taking over from civil
servants and why we need to worry about it

Alasdair Palmer

CIVITAS

First Published November 2015

© Civitas 2015
55 Tufton Street
London SW1P 3QL

email: books@civitas.org.uk

ISBN 978-1-906837-73-0

Independence: Civitas: Institute for the Study of Civil Society is a registered educational charity (No. 1085494) and a company limited by guarantee (No. 04023541). Civitas is financed from a variety of private sources to avoid over-reliance on any single or small group of donors.

All publications are independently refereed. All the Institute's publications seek to further its objective of promoting the advancement of learning. The views expressed are those of the authors, not of the Institute, as is responsibility for data and content.

Designed and typeset by
lukejefford.com

Printed in Great Britain by
Berforts Group Ltd
Stevenage, SGI 2BH

Contents

Author

Alasdair Palmer was born in London and read history and philosophy at Cambridge. He has worked for Granada Television (now ITV), *The Spectator* and *The Sunday Telegraph*, where he won the Charles Douglas Home Prize for Journalism in 2002. He has been a creative consultant for HBO in Los Angeles and spent 18 months at the Home Office as a civil servant, observing the relationship between ministers, special advisers and civil servants while writing speeches for Theresa May. He currently is writing a television drama series about human rights with Peter Berry. He is married with two children.

Acknowledgements

A number of people read and made helpful comments on this report prior to its publication. The author would particularly like to thank Daniel Bentley, Simon Berthon, Amy Erickson, Peter Hennessy, Peter Morris, Brian Palmer, Alan Petty, Mark Thompson, Jonathan Sumption, Daniel Wolf and David Wood. He would also like to thank David Green for commissioning the report, and for his consistent encouragement.

Introduction

No Sir Humphrey

The procedures of government do not receive the discussion they deserve. They are critically important. They make the difference between effective government and government that is oppressive and corrupt. But they do not seem to interest the electorate, or at least the portion of it that influences what is on television and in the newspapers – and as a consequence, procedures of government are rarely the focus of attention.

Yet there is an increasing consensus amongst historians, political scientists and even economists that the most important step for achieving and maintaining a free and prosperous society is getting administrative procedures right: ensuring that they are cost-effective and run by politicians and officials who do not view public office as a means to making as much money as possible for themselves and their supporters.[1]

Historically, uncorrupt and efficient government has been rare. It is still rare in most of the world today. Politicians and officials in many countries see political power as giving them a great advantage which they can and should use for their own personal benefit. Britain's heritage of relatively uncorrupt government, with officials who see it as their role to ensure that 'ministers of any persuasion will not be able to use the machinery of the state to personal or party political advantage',[2] is as remarkable as it is precious.

That heritage is largely the result of the reforms inspired by the 1854 report from civil servants Sir Stafford Northcote and Charles Trevelyan. Their proposals were, for the time, revolutionary: they advocated ending the time-honoured tradition that government employment should be based on nepotism and jobbery. They identified political patronage as a sure way of generating incompetent government. They thought most of the problems with the way Britain was governed derived from the fact that its officials were appointed not because they were the best person for the job, but because they were a friend or relative of someone in political power. As a result, government bureaucracy was staffed by what the Northcote-Trevelyan Report described as 'the unambitious, the indolent or the incapable'.

To ensure that the right people were given posts in government – people, that is, who were capable of performing the tasks effectively and efficiently, and who would not be corrupt – it was essential to take the appointments process out of the hands of politicians, and give it to a politically independent organisation that would offer government posts to individuals solely on the basis of an assessment of their being the most capable candidate available. That is why they thought that meritocratic appointments required that those in charge of making them should be committed to the values of objectivity and impartiality. If the people doing the appointing were tied to any particular political party, then party considerations would inevitably end up determining appointments. And that would ensure that the wrong people were appointed, which in turn would produce inefficient, and probably corrupt, government.

2

To replace this system, they recommended the creation of a civil service free of all taint of political patronage, whose members were selected wholly on the basis of merit, and who would be trained to reflect the values of impartiality and objectivity which Northcote and Trevelyan thought were necessary for the preparation and selection of rational and effective government policies.

Practices deriving from Northcote's and Trevelyan's reforms have characterised the British civil service for well over a century. But they are not self-sustaining: they require commitment, care and attention from politicians and officials if they are to be carried on. We could easily do things differently, with much less emphasis on the political independence of the civil service, and with far less use for its objective and impartial scrutiny of political policies. In the United States, many thousands of officials are changed whenever a presidential election produces a president from a different party. The system of political appointments is known as 'the spoils system', after President Jackson, who was elected in 1829 and wanted to replace the existing officials with ones that were politically sympathetic to him: he justified his action by saying bluntly 'to the victor, the spoils'. Nearly 150 years later, President Eisenhower cemented that approach to government office when he issued an executive order ensuring that only his political supporters could be employed in positions that involved providing policy advice or reading confidential documents.[3] We could follow the same model here. But very few people with experience of both systems think that it would be an improvement.

My contention in this pamphlet is that we are moving slowly but surely in that direction, and in a typically

British fashion. No-one in power has announced it. No-one in power has even admitted it. The political rhetoric from ministers of all three main parties has been to insist that the Northcote-Trevelyan settlement is being preserved, that they value and want to keep the benefits of policy advice that can only come from independent and impartial officials. But the actions of successive governments since 1997 have in fact been to downgrade and marginalise objective and impartial civil service advice, and to replace it with counsel from politically committed special advisers.

Because the rhetoric is so different from the reality, it is not easy to work out exactly what is going on. Many academic commentators seem to me to have been misled by the statements and regulations in favour of impartial and objective advice provided by permanent officials into thinking that the statements on paper represent the reality. In the testimony given to the numerous parliamentary select committees that have written reports on the civil service over the last 15 years, and in the books and pamphlets that have been written by special advisers themselves, it is possible to unearth evidence that something very different has been happening.

I also had the experience of seeing something of the way government now works at first hand when I was employed as a civil servant to write speeches for Theresa May at the Home Office. I expected the Home Office to be a version of *Yes Minister*, the television show that, thirty years ago, so effectively portrayed wily, omniscient civil servants manipulating dim politicians. It was not in the least like that: however accurate it might have been when it was first broadcast, *Yes Minister* is a completely misleading portrayal of how government works today. Far from being manipulated by senior civil servants, the secretary of state and her special advisers had an enormously powerful influence on the department. Advice from impartial and objective civil servants was much less important than straightforwardly political counsel from the unquestionably extremely able special advisers.

Did what seemed to be the marginalisation of civil service advice mean that worse decisions were being taken? That is obviously the critical issue. Unfortunately, I was not in a position to make a judgement on it. All that I can say with any confidence is that the process of diminishing the role of objective, impartial scrutiny of policy proposals was well under way. That is not necessarily a harbinger of a precipitous decline in administrative standards. But there is a serious risk that it could be. Lord (Peter) Hennessy once correctly observed that good government is 'like a clean water supply – you take no notice of it until it is contaminated, by which time it is too late'.[4] The practice of good government in Britain has not been lost – yet. But it is changing, and in ways which could eventually lead to the disappearance of objective and impartial scrutiny of government policy by civil service officials prior to that policy being implemented. We need a keener awareness that we could be in danger of losing it, because without one, we could soon wake up to find that it is gone.[5]

1

Impartiality, objectivity, honesty and integrity

Every minister who speaks publicly about the civil service praises its values of impartiality, objectivity, honesty and integrity. Although they may think the civil service needs reform, they rarely openly proclaim that its faults are related to its commitment to those values. It is almost universally recognised that impartiality, objectivity, honesty and integrity are essential qualities of good government officials. Those values are, along with the selection of officials on the basis of merit alone, regarded as the bedrock of an effective civil service.

The essential characteristic of special advisers is that they are *not* committed to impartiality and objectivity: that, and the fact that they are not selected on merit alone, is what distinguishes them from the permanent officials of the civil service.

So why do many ministers – and many commentators, academic and otherwise – think that effective government is now impossible without special advisers?[1] Ministers stress that they need advice and help from people who are emphatically not impartial and objective. They believe they need advisers whose priority is to get the party manifesto that won the election implemented. Objective and impartial officials are not as good at this as politically partisan advisers who have been selected because ministers know they can rely on them to support their political programme.

Why would ministers believe that objectivity and impartiality constitute a bar, or at least a handicap, to the effective implementation of party policies? Do they think that their own policies cannot stand up to impartial and objective scrutiny, and if they receive too much of it, serious faults and inadequacies will be exposed? That is surely not the reason why ministers think they need to go outside the civil service for advice. Ministers' conviction that they need politically engaged advisers rather springs from a generalised distrust of Whitehall officials, and of their claims to assess policies impartially and objectively.

That distrust cuts across both main political parties. Underlying it is the conviction that political policies cannot be effectively implemented by politically neutral – that is impartial – officials. Many politicians have the sense that the much-vaunted impartiality of the civil service is a myth. Civil servants inevitably have their own views on what should be done, and whatever those views are, sooner or later they are bound to conflict with what the elected government has a mandate to do. Few critics of civil service impartiality would be as blunt as Charles Clarke, who, in the course of a discussion about the civil service's values of objectivity and impartiality, stated: 'I do not fit the description of "totally objective" to anything. I do not believe such a thing exists. I think it is a nonsensical concept.'[2]

But many would agree that civil servants' commitment to impartiality and objectivity can get in the way of their implementing government policy effectively. Francis Maude, who was the Coalition's Cabinet Office minister, and in charge of civil service reform, has even gone so far as to suggest that it may be time to diminish the civil service's commitment to impartiality, objectivity, honesty and integrity. While recognising that those values are 'really important', Maude also stressed that they are 'static, passive values. And two are essentially mirrors of the others'. He described the 'great virtues' as 'pace, professionalism, passion, pride', adding that 'they're warm, dynamic, human' – as opposed, presumably, to the cold and inhuman values of impartiality, objectivity, integrity and honesty.[3]

Even Oliver Letwin, minister for government policy under the Coalition, who is in many ways a defender of the traditional values of the civil service, indicated deep anxiety about permanent officials' lack of enthusiasm for policies that ministers have a mandate from the electorate to implement. In a speech on civil service reform, Letwin asserted: 'Administrative civil servants can, at their worst, defeat ministerial objectives just by ensuring that when the minister has decided to act, nothing actually happens. Such failures of transmission are the enemies of democracy – and one of the things that our civil service reform programme is designed to do is to eliminate such failures.'[4]

In 1959, perhaps the high-water mark of respect for the British civil service, C.H. Sisson wrote in *The Spirit of British Administration*:

> The argument for taking more political control of the civil service is that permanent officials cannot be trusted to share the enthusiasm of politicians, and that they will be less effective advisers and executants than men who share the ministers' political convictions and ambitions.

Sisson, who spent 30 years as a civil servant, and whose book is a paean of praise to the British civil service, dismissed that argument as 'rarely held by the politician who has experience of office'.[5] Perhaps that was true in 1959. It is certainly not true in 2015. But Sisson accurately sums up the politician's case for special advisers: the effective implementation of any politically controversial policy requires not objectivity and impartiality, but political commitment. Many ministers have stressed this point – for example Lord (Andrew) Adonis, who was a special adviser to Tony Blair before he was appointed education minister, then transport secretary. Lord Adonis insisted to the Public Administration Committee that the trouble with permanent civil servants is that 'there is not this intense passion [for the elected government's policies] that there needs to be'.[6]

Special advisers were first introduced as a counterweight to what was perceived as the civil service's lack of enthusiasm and commitment by Harold Wilson in 1964.[7] The economist Nicholas Kaldor was one of two outside experts (the other was the economist Thomas Balogh) who were hired by Wilson's administration. Their purpose, in Kaldor's words, was 'to conduct Labour ministers' battles with the civil service... [because] the civil service gradually develops its own set of views and is an autonomous body, which on the whole is naturally conservative'. Balogh had also claimed in *The Apotheosis of the Dilettante*, a highly critical look at the condition of the civil service, that officials conspired to enforce an orthodox economic policy agenda on ministers, with the result that Labour's socialist economic platform was inevitably frustrated when it was left to civil servants to implement it.[8]

The 1964 Labour government's experiment with special advisers was not an unqualified success. Kaldor and Balogh felt they were under-used. Harold Wilson (who had himself been a civil servant during the war) retained a belief that relying on 'loyal civil servants' produced better results than replacing them with outsiders. But Wilson's use of special advisers as a way of getting around what was perceived as the reluctance, or the inability, of permanent officials to implement the policies of the elected government was a harbinger of things to come. It began a trend which, over time, has gathered great force. After Labour won the election held on 28 February 1974, Wilson increased the number of special advisers to 30. Each cabinet minister was authorised to employ a maximum of two. Wilson himself set up his own policy unit of seven people with, as he put it, 'expert knowledge in the fields of economic, industrial and social policy... The policy unit was set up, and its members selected, to provide a team with strong political commitment to... further the government's political goals'.[9]

In 1964 Wilson's special advisers were experts in their field of economics: both Kaldor and Balogh had considerable academic reputations. But over the next 50 years, special advisers have come to be younger and less expert, often being hired in their twenties within a few years of graduation. The idea that enthusiasm and commitment are more important qualities in an adviser than expertise seems to have originated with George Lansbury, Labour's leader after Ramsay MacDonald became head of the National government in 1931. Lansbury argued that if Labour were elected, it would need to place people at the top of all government departments who accepted Labour's social and economic policies and were wholeheartedly determined to make them successful. He thought the political commitment of those appointed was going to be much more important than their administrative skills: it was their beliefs rather than their knowledge that mattered.[10]

Clement Attlee, the Labour leader swept to power in the election of July 1945, took a more benign view of the civil service, and was more willing to appreciate the value of its expertise. But to judge by the age and qualifications of those who have been selected as special advisers over the past two decades, both major parties have come to share Lansbury's judgement that political commitment is more important than administrative experience. The median age of special advisers declined from 36 under John Major's administration to 31 under the Coalition. The number of advisers appointed because they have expert knowledge of a technical subject such as arms control has also diminished.[11] The tendency, as Lord Hennessy has stressed, has been to employ people as special advisers because of what they believe, rather than because of what they know.

Why? Why has political commitment been preferred to proven expertise? That choice makes perfect sense if the problem needing solution is regarded as the impartiality and objectivity of officials: their professional lack of political commitment is necessary for them to be able to provide continuity, and to serve whichever government is elected; but it may make them professionally unable to implement a new elected government's priorities with the enthusiasm and alacrity that a new minister taking control of a department would wish. Expertise is not something in short supply in Whitehall, and if officials themselves are not expert in a particular field, it is not difficult for them to get access to people who are. What officials lack, and are supposed to lack, is political commitment. Francis Maude, when he was Cabinet Office minister and paymaster general, insisted:

> The principal benefit of special advisers, certainly for me and for other ministers I think, is to have highly intelligent people about whom there can never be any suggestion of divided loyalties. That is really important.[12]

Note the assumption inherent in Maude's statement: officials are likely to have divided loyalties – they are not going to be wholly dedicated to the political priorities of the elected government in the way that special advisers, chosen at least partly for their political commitment, will be. Maude added that one of the critical roles of special advisers was 'to ensure that the decisions that have been taken [by the minister] are actually implemented in the way that was intended'. He was very clear: 'I do not think that the best use for a special adviser is to provide subject expertise.'

An indication of just how worried ministers have become by what they perceive to be officials' lack of engagement in the elected government's priorities is the almost hysterical reaction to the discovery of a civil service document which specified the qualities needed to fill the job of permanent secretary. It was written in 2009, but Francis Maude didn't see it until July 2014. He was shocked to discover that the document, entitled 'Indicators of Potential for Permanent Secretary Roles', had a sentence stating that a permanent secretary should be able to 'balance ministers' or high level stakeholders' immediate needs or priorities with the long-term aims of their department'. The document also stated that suitable candidates should be able to cope with 'often irrational demands'.

Maude said that the document 'does not conform to constitutional propriety', on the grounds that he thought that it implied that officials are not obliged to follow government policy. Nick Herbert, who had been a minister at the Ministry of Justice, opined that it was an 'extraordinary document':

> This is actually beyond a joke. We can't have a kind of permanent government of an unelected bureaucracy deciding that it has its own long-term priorities which may be different to those of ministers and the elected government.[13]

But of course, that is not what the document asserts or implies. And furthermore, the civil service *does* inevitably, and uncontroversially, have its own long-term priorities which may be different to those of ministers and the elected government. For instance: the civil service is responsible for maintaining continuity, and ensuring that government can continue in an uninterrupted fashion between administrations and during periods of transition. Although, as citizens, ministers probably have an interest in seeing that the civil service performs that function, as party politicians, they may not do so. At any event, it is unlikely to be high on their list of priorities. But it is and ought to be high on the list of any permanent secretary's. And if a minister's priorities were to involve dismantling his or her department's ability to continue to function over the long term, then quite rightly it would be a permanent secretary's job to 'balance' those ministerial demands against the long-term interests of the department in maintaining a continued ability to perform its role effectively.

That Maude and Herbert see a Whitehall conspiracy to frustrate the aims of the elected government in a bland statement of what is indisputably part of a permanent secretary's job indicates the extent to which the civil service has lost the trust of many elected politicians. Civil servants can and no doubt do frustrate ministers by their failure to implement their ministers' preferred policies fast enough or even at all. But this document cannot be accurately interpreted as encouraging that kind of behaviour.

The political engagement of special advisers is not only advocated as a way of combatting the professional scepticism, and occasionally what is perceived as the hostility, or even just the plain indolence, of officials towards the effective implementation of the political policies of the elected government. Perhaps because they are aware that criticising the civil service for too great a commitment to impartiality and objectivity is not good politics (no-one, or almost no-one, comes out *against* impartiality and objectivity when discussing what virtues it is rational to want permanent officials to exhibit), ministers have come up with another explanation for why they need special advisers. Far from undermining the values of objectivity and impartiality, they maintain, special advisers are the best way of protecting the civil service's commitment to them.

Ministers are obviously politicians as well as administrators in charge of departments. They have party political tasks they have to perform: for instance, convincing members of their own party that the policies they are following are consistent with the political ideals of the party they represent. Special advisers are engaged to perform the political tasks that a minister needs done, or needs advice and help with, so that permanent officials do not have to be implicated in that process, and can therefore remain objective and impartial. This is stated explicitly in the first paragraph of the 2010 Code of Conduct for Special Advisers:

> The employment of special advisers adds a political dimension to the advice and assistance available to ministers, while reinforcing the political impartiality of the permanent civil service by distinguishing the source of political advice and support.

The second paragraph states:

> Special advisers are employed to help ministers on matters where the work of the government and the work of the government party overlap, and where it would be inappropriate for permanent civil servants to become involved.

The underlying logic of that claim is perfectly sound: politically motivated special advisers, chosen because of their political commitments, will, by performing politically sensitive or partisan tasks, protect the civil service from entanglement in party political issues. Permanent officials do not have to compromise their objectivity and impartiality: issues which require political commitment are handled by the minister's own political appointees. Put like that, it sounds a wholly benign process, and one that is beneficial to all concerned, including the citizens of this country – which may be why a large number of senior civil servants accept it.

The difficulty is that it is not at all easy to locate the line that separates the tasks for which political commitment is required. Any individual chosen for ministerial office is selected as the representative of a political party. The policies they are expected to implement derive in large part from the political programme of the political party that won the last election. Elected politicians' recurrent complaint about the civil service usually amounts to the allegation that *because* civil service officials do not share their (the elected government's) political commitments, they do not, and perhaps cannot, implement its policies with the alacrity and effectiveness that is required.

That argument is distorted when made into an all-or-nothing proposition. It would not be true to claim that most politicians want immediately to replace all of the senior civil service with a group of officials appointed wholly on grounds of their political allegiance. It would also be false to claim that there is no role for advisers whose role is explicitly political, and who perform roles that civil servants should not – such as, for example, liaising between the minister and his party, or briefing journalists on the politics of the minister's policies, or advising on suitable material for a speech at the annual party conference.

The question is rather one of degree. Politicians can see the benefits of a permanent civil service, committed to the objective and impartial assessment of policies: they certainly *say* they can see those benefits often enough. But they also have a keen sense of its costs. Given that elected politicians perceive a conflict between getting the policies they have been elected to put into practice implemented quickly and effectively and having those policies evaluated, criticised and then implemented by officials committed to impartiality and objectivity, the issue is the balance between the two goals. How much of the department's policy business is best handled by people who are politically committed rather than by those who are professionally impartial and objective?

2

'This is shit': The marginalisation of civil servants

If ministers think that most policy business, whether it is advice or implementation, needs politically committed people if it is to be done effectively, then the consequence of insulating civil service officials from political tasks will inevitably be to marginalise their role.[1] That is precisely what Sir Robin Mountfield, who was permanent secretary at the Cabinet Office for five years from 1995 to 1999, thought he had observed happening. In 2002 he wrote: 'My own view is that the greatest threat the special advisers in their present form pose to the civil service is not the politicisation of civil servants, but their marginalisation in the advice process.'[2] Lord (Andrew) Turnbull, who was cabinet secretary and head of the civil service from 2002 to 2005, said in 2008:

> More [civil service work] goes through the minister's special adviser channel than used to be the case. I think ministers still respect the political neutrality of the civil service, but they do not use it to the extent that they used to, or that they should. [3]

Sir Richard Mottram, who was permanent secretary at a number of different departments, including the Ministry of Defence and the Cabinet Office, made basically the same point when he insisted that, rather than ministers 'actively seeking to undermine the political impartiality of the civil service', what 'has been happening… is that ministers give relatively less weight to the contribution of the civil service in the formulation of policy and in advising generally.' He added: 'There has been a developing trend towards giving more weight to the role of special advisers, and that has speeded up.' He felt that a pressing question for members of both Houses of Parliament was how far they 'wish that trend to continue'.[4]

Is it correct to maintain that special advisers are gradually taking over the civil service's role in providing policy advice to ministers? The answer to that question is of considerable importance. Moving from a situation in which policies are primarily assessed by officials committed to impartiality and objectivity before they are implemented, and are amended on the basis of that assessment, to one where the primary assessment is done by politically engaged individuals, would be a very significant change in the way this country is governed. It is not obvious that it is a change that we as citizens and taxpayers want to happen. And if it is happening, it is happening without discussion or consultation: you will not find a commitment to diminish the role of impartial and objective civil service advice on policy in any party manifesto.

So how much influence on policy-making do special advisers have? There is one bad argument to the effect that they have very little. The argument is essentially based on numbers: the number of special advisers is small while the number of civil servants is huge – therefore, special advisers cannot have much influence. When he was prime minister, Tony Blair made this point to the Commons Liaison Committee on 16 July 2002. 'We have 80 special advisers for the whole government', he said. 'There are 3,500 senior civil servants... I think we need to get this in context.'[5] In 2005, in a debate in the Lords, Lord (Gus) Macdonald of Tradeston, who from 2001 to 2003 was Cabinet Office minister, claimed:

> Surely no serious commentator imagines that a small band of about 80 special advisers – only one, Jonathan Powell, with executive authority – has somehow become an agency with the power and intent to threaten the integrity and tradition of 3,900 senior civil servants.[6]

Similarly, in their written evidence to the Public Administration Select Committee in May 2012, Professors David Richards and Martin Smith, together with the former special adviser Patrick Diamond, insisted:

> The notion that Whitehall has been marginalised by the relative growth of spads [special advisers]... is both a misrepresentation and a misunderstanding of the role played by spads in the British political system. Indeed, in terms of numbers and relative influence, there are very few special advisers in relation to permanent civil servants.[7]

Even senior civil servants put this argument. For instance, Lord (Richard) Wilson, when he gave evidence to the Public Administration Select Committee (PASC) in 2000 – he was then cabinet secretary – maintained: '70-odd advisers could not swamp the senior civil service of 3,700 people.'[8]

The problem with the numbers argument is that it rests on a fallacy. It is simply not true to conclude that if x is smaller in number than y, then x has less influence than y. Obviously, in any organisation with a command structure, from an army or a government to a business, there are a few people at the top, and many people at the bottom: the many outnumber the few, but the few at the top have far greater influence on what action the organisation takes. There is only one prime minister or chief executive or field marshal, but their decisions determine what actions the organisation that they lead will take, in a way that those of their much more numerous underlings do not. Having insisted to PASC that the small number of special advisers precluded them from having greater influence than civil servants on policy advice, Richard Wilson sent a diagram depicting how Number 10's staff was organised which showed Jonathan Powell – a special adviser, not a career civil servant – at its apex. In answer to the question, 'Is Jonathan Powell in charge at Number 10?', the then cabinet secretary replied: 'Yes.'[9]

So the question about the extent of the influence of special advisers cannot be answered just by looking at their numbers – although in fact these have grown consistently since 1997. When Tony Blair was elected prime minister, he brought more than 70 special advisers with him, doubling the number John Major had used, who in turn had more than Margaret Thatcher. Every government since Tony Blair resigned in 2007 has promised to reduce the number of special advisers. Every government has ended up increasing them. It is almost certain David Cameron will not end his second term in office with fewer special advisers than he had before the 2015 election.

It is perfectly consistent with there being fewer special advisers than senior civil servants that special advisers should increasingly determine what policy advice ministers receive. Do they in fact do this? It is not easy to get reliable evidence on the matter. Civil servants who are currently employed, as opposed to retired, are not usually allowed, under the terms of their contract, to speak publicly about their employment and what they see happening in their department. Special advisers are bound by the same obligation not to disclose anything whilst in employment. But because their positions are usually temporary, more of them have written and spoken after leaving the role. In evidence to parliament's select committees, they have tended to insist that – as Michael Jacobs, a special adviser to Gordon Brown from 2004 to 2010, told PASC in 2012 – 'the idea that in some sense advisers "usurp" or "marginalize" the role of civil servants is mistaken'.[10]

There are grounds, however, for thinking that evidence given by former special advisers on this topic to parliamentary committees is not always wholly reliable. For example, Paul Richards, who was a special adviser to Hazel Blears, told the Lords Constitution Committee: 'The idea that a spad would tell a civil servant what to do is nonsense. I never experienced that with myself or anyone else.'[11] It was then pointed out to him that in 1997, Jonathan Powell and Alastair Campbell, two of Tony Blair's special advisers, were specifically given the power to command civil service officials by orders in council. Richards accepted that yes, that had happened.[12] But he said it was merely a 'one-off, a blip if you will' – although one that, in Powell's case, lasted for over a decade. His power to command civil servants was not rescinded until 2007, when

Gordon Brown became prime minister and Jonathan Powell left Number 10 with Tony Blair.

In his memoirs of his time as Tony Blair's chief of staff, Jonathan Powell maintains that the measure formally confirming his power to give orders to civil servants wasn't necessary. Powell is emphatic that it was 'ludicrous... to suggest that we [Powell and Campbell] were doing anything different from what Ed Balls was doing in the Treasury as a special adviser to Gordon Brown or other special advisers were doing elsewhere in Whitehall'.[13] That is: all special advisers give orders to civil servants – so nothing whatever was gained by giving the two most senior special advisers the formal power to do this.

In 2002, the Public Administration Select Committee conducted an inquiry into the 'Jo Moore affair'.[14] Jo Moore was the special adviser at the Department of Transport who sent an email on 11 September 2001, suggesting it was a good day to 'get out anything we want to bury: councillors' expenses?' She made the same point five months later, on 14 February 2002, the day of Princess Margaret's funeral. In the course of examining her actions, the committee noted: 'Ms Moore took on a series of executive and in effect managerial tasks without reference to the proper procedures.' It is striking that no-one in a position to take action seems to have tried to do anything to stop her taking on 'executive and managerial tasks'– a phrase that serves as a euphemism for giving civil servants orders. It did not even generate any comment until after she was caught trying to bury bad news by getting it out on the day of the 9/11 attacks and of Princess Margaret's funeral. What was thought outrageous about Jo Moore's conduct as a special adviser was not that she took on 'executive and… managerial tasks'. It was that she sent those emails.

This seems to me strong evidence that special advisers under Blair were indeed doing routinely what Jonathan Powell insists that they were: that is, giving commands to civil servants. Lord (Richard) Wilson, who was cabinet secretary from 1998-2002, denied that this happened when giving evidence to the Committee on Standards in Public Life in 2002. Sir Malcolm Wicks asked him if special advisers gave 'instructions' to civil servants. Lord Wilson replied that he thought 'direct orders are relatively rare'. He maintained the usual situation was that 'you have a discussion about it… I think that is a much more common situation than someone banging the table, as the word 'instructions' implies, and giving an order.'[15]

But Lord Wilson would not have been party to the typical interactions between a special adviser and a junior or mid-ranking civil servant. It may well have been the case that for a civil servant as elevated as the cabinet secretary, who is also head of the whole home civil service, meetings with special advisers did not involve special advisers issuing 'instructions'. Further down the food chain, however, the relationship between special advisers and civil servants was unlikely to have been quite so collegial.

Civil servants rarely complain publicly about their conditions of employment: doing so is effectively career suicide. However, evidence occasionally surfaces that suggests that at lower levels, relations can involve special advisers banging the table – sometimes metaphorically, sometimes not – in the process of giving orders to civil servants. For example, at the Treasury, Shriti Vadera, one of Gordon Brown's special advisers, was famous for reducing junior civil servants to tears, and shouting at them so much that she earned the nickname 'Shriti the Shriek'.[16] A civil servant who alleged that she was bullied and intimidated by special advisers at the Department for Education agreed to a settlement prior to the case reaching an industrial tribunal, but some of its details were nevertheless reported.[17] Those are obviously extreme cases. How representative they are of the general run of special adviser behaviour is difficult to assess, and I shall not attempt to do so. My point is that whether it is done politely or aggressively, special advisers give orders to civil servants.

Concerns about the extent to which special advisers were assuming de facto management functions over career civil servants surfaced in a debate in the Lords on 1 May 2002. They came up in a report of the Committee on Standards in Public Life, 'Defining the Boundaries within the Executive: Ministers, Special Advisers and the permanent Civil Service'. Tony Blair responded to those anxieties by making a change to the Code of Conduct for Special Advisers that removed their power to 'instruct' civil servants. It is not clear whether this had any effect. At any rate, when he became prime minister in 2007 Gordon Brown felt it was necessary once again to remove any power special advisers might have had to give civil servants commands.

Did that finally make sure that special advisers were not able to give commands to civil servants? What happens in reality does not automatically follow what an order in council says should happen. If Jonathan Powell is correct in maintaining that it was quite unnecessary to give him, as a special adviser, the formal power through an order in council to give instructions to civil servants, it follows that nothing was lost when that power was formally rescinded in 2007. Which means we can expect a degree of continuity between the powers that Powell says all special advisers exercised over permanent officials during the Blair years, and the powers that they have exercised over civil servants since then. Has the situation in fact changed in the years since 2007? Charles Clarke told the Lords Constitution Committee in 2012:

> There were examples, certainly in the last Labour government, of senior ministers who took key policy decisions closeted with their special advisers and... were not ready to allow civil servants to comment on them. Some current ministers [in the then Coalition government] do that too.[18]

Nick Hillman, who was special adviser to the universities and science minister David Willetts, has stressed that when their minister was absent for whatever reason, 'special advisers become the voice, as well as the eyes and ears, of their minister at many internal government meetings... In such periods, special advisers can also become the main (rather than the initial) point of call for clearing parliamentary questions, ministerial correspondence, and comments for the press'.[19] That is to say: they give instructions to civil servants. Dominic Cummings, who was special adviser to Michael Gove at the Department for Education, states on his blog:

> Most of my job was converting long-term goals into reality *via* policy, operational planning, and project management. This requires focus on daily, weekly, monthly, and quarterly steps, and management to make sure people are doing what is needed to get there.

The 'people' that Cummings refers to here are civil servants: he clearly felt it was part of his job to manage them.[20]

I have spoken to a number of civil servants, mostly at mid-levels of seniority, about the power of special advisers. Unfortunately, their contract prevents them from talking publicly about their employment, so I cannot identify them. But they were unanimous in saying the special advisers had a great deal of power, both over civil servants and over what sort of advice the minister received: one was even explicit that he had seen 'many senior civil servants' careers ruined because they cannot get on with spads'. I observed special advisers giving orders to civil servants when I was employed as a civil servant (rather than a special adviser) to write speeches for Theresa May at the Home Office. They certainly gave orders to me.

How can this happen? How can special advisers be in a position to give orders to permanent civil servants? Particularly given that the Code of Conduct for Special Advisers specifically states that 'special advisers must not... exercise any power in relation to the management of any part of the civil service'? One part of the explanation is that the code also states that special advisers 'may, on behalf of their ministers: convey ministers' views and work priorities; request officials to prepare and provide information and data, including analyses and papers; hold meetings with officials to discuss the advice being put to ministers'.

Special advisers are chosen personally by the minister for whom they work. They have a very close relationship with that minister. They have direct and unfettered access to him or her in a way that civil servants, with the exception of the prime minister's principal private secretary and the department's permanent secretary, do not. They can claim to represent the minister and to speak for him or her. The anodyne phrase 'convey to officials ministers' views and work priorities' does not quite communicate the authority that special advisers derive from being able to claim to be the minister's representative – which is an accurate description of what they are. That role gives them an ability to command civil servants that goes far beyond merely 'requesting' anything. Special advisers can say that they are not violating the code because it is not *they* who are doing the commanding: it is the minister, who is of course entitled to command civil servants, for a civil servant's role is to serve their minister. Because they insist they are merely the means through which the minister's 'requests' are conveyed, special advisers can claim, when issuing orders to civil servants, to be acting in a way that is completely legitimate.

Ministers are aware of this, and can be presumed to endorse it. It is significant that in 2005, the code of conduct was altered so that the role of special adviser was changed from 'giving advice only' to ministers, and replaced with 'providing assistance' to ministers – which is a far broader, and much less specific, role. In a debate on the matter in the Lords on 7 November 2005, Lord Macdonald, the former Cabinet Office minister, stated he welcomed 'the recent change in the civil service order in council to formalise what was always blindingly obvious: namely, that the key role of special advisers is to give more than advice to ministers; it is give assistance'. He added that 'such assistance can encompass conveying instructions and commissioning works'.[21] Lord Macdonald would have been aware that in 2003, Tony Blair had altered the Code of Conduct for

Special Advisers to delete the power to 'instruct' civil servants. He clearly did not think it made a material difference to their powers. Gordon Brown, as prime minister, pushed through the Constitutional Reform and Governance Act 2010, which put the civil service, for the first time, on a statutory footing. That act confirmed the description of the special adviser's role as 'providing assistance to the minister'.

While the giving of 'assistance' to ministers may formally describe what special advisers do, it does not capture the power that it gives them over civil servants. As far as I can tell, the Joint Committee on the Constitutional Reform Bill (it became the Constitutional Reform and Governance Act) is the only parliamentary committee to have noticed that there could be a problem with the description of a special advisers' purpose as to 'assist a minister'. The committee observed that '"assist" [is] a flexible definition that suggests any number of possible tasks may be permissible'. As a consequence, 'the Code of Conduct for Special Advisers provides for special advisers to exercise what are in effect management functions over career officials, such as communicating instructions from ministers and asking them to take on tasks'. It recommended that the code be 'clarified to rule out managerial functions'.[22]

The code has indeed been modified in a way which, in theory, rules out special advisers having managerial functions over permanent officials. But their purpose, as defined by the code, remains to 'assist' ministers, and they may 'convey ministers' views and work priorities'. The result? In practice, special advisers' managerial powers over civil servants remain. Nor does the phrase 'give assistance to ministers' reflect the extent to which they can marginalise the advice provided to ministers by permanent civil servants.

The Code of Conduct for Special Advisers states that special advisers 'must not suppress or supplant the advice being prepared for ministers by permanent civil servants, although they may comment on such advice'. I suppose writing 'This is shit' in the margin (as one special adviser notoriously used to do at the Home Office) counts as a comment on advice, rather than suppressing or supplanting it. But special advisers are uniquely well-placed to suppress or supplant advice from civil servants. As Paul Richards, who was special adviser to Hazel Blears at the Department for Communities and Local Government, emphasised in his evidence to the Lords Constitution Committee: 'The special adviser reads everything that goes into the [minister's] red box. They have the prerogative to write a covering note on top of everything.' This obviously places them in a position of great power, because as Lord (Charles) Powell (who, as a civil servant, was Margaret Thatcher's private secretary on foreign affairs) noted, 'we all know that the last voice is the one that counts most'.[23]

There is, as far as I can ascertain, no direct evidence – there's no formal admission or statement - that special advisers suppress or supplant advice from civil servants. The closest that a (former) special adviser gets to admitting doing this is when Nick Hillman states that he regularly inserted into David Willetts' red box papers that had failed the regular civil service clearing process: that is, papers which senior permanent officials had decided should *not* go forward to the minister, because those officials thought they weren't significant enough to bother him with. Hillman recalls that he read those 'non-papers', and if *he* thought any of them were sufficiently interesting, he made sure that David Willetts saw them.[24] If Hillman thought he could legitimately *include* material that officials thought David Willetts should *not* see, he presumably also thought he could *exclude* material that those officials thought David Willetts *should* be given. I do not know whether he actually did this, but it would be very surprising if special advisers were not occasionally tempted to suppress or supplant advice from civil servants, and did not, once in a while, give in to that temptation. But it is hard for anyone else to know when, or if, that has happened. Lord Turnbull, in his evidence to the Joint Committee on the Constitutional Reform Bill, indicated that he thought it had been happening, which is why he had written into the Code of Conduct for Special Advisers that they should not suppress or supplant civil service advice. Special advisers, he insisted, 'should not get into a position where they try to dictate what goes to the minister and what does not – and I think that has been the case in recent years.'[25]

The issue is not whether special advisers are talented, able, diligent and provide their ministers with good advice. The issue is simply that however good their advice is, it is *not* impartial or objective. The whole point of having special advisers is that they should be politically engaged. If they are gradually, but effectively, marginalising and supplanting advice from civil servants, the result would eventually be to change the way in which we are governed. It would be to undo the 1854 Northcote-Trevelyan Report, which established the principle that elected politicians in positions of executive authority should be advised principally by impartial and objective civil servants selected on merit, not on the basis of ministerial patronage – which is how special advisers are chosen. To repeat: the marginalisation of civil service advice is a process, and one which happens by degrees. The civil service has never had a monopoly on providing policy advice to ministers, and nor should it. But it is important that policy proposals, wherever they come from, are subjected to the objective and impartial scrutiny which the current civil service was set up to provide.

I am not claiming that the civil service has been politicised: permanent civil servants are still appointed on merit, not patronage, and the culture of honesty, objectivity and impartiality is alive and well within the civil service. I *am* claiming that the process of giving advice to ministers is being politicised, with the result that ministers do not get the amount of objective, impartial advice from permanent officials that they used to. The result is not, or not yet, the elimination of all objective and impartial advice on policy from the civil service. It is its steady diminution, to the point where it can be seriously questioned whether the policies that are in fact implemented have been modified by that impartial and objective advice.

There are two factors which combine to produce that result. One is the power that special advisers derive from their closeness to their minister, which enables them to intervene directly to dictate what civil servants do and what the minister sees. The other is their capacity to intimidate civil servants, especially junior and mid-ranking ones, by the way in which they use the authority that they have as their minister's representative. Special advisers do not often admit that they have the power to do this. But Giles Wilkes, who was Vince Cable's special adviser from 2010 to 2014, does so when he reflects that special advisers' 'ability to cow civil servants does not imply a similar ability to bend reality'. That statement, made in the context of a discussion of how special advisers 'need to do more than just find an idea they like and aggressively push it through', indicates that Wilkes thinks that intimidating civil servants can be a routine part of the way that many special advisers operate.

All the civil servants that I spoke to – and they were all junior or mid-ranking rather than senior – maintained that the special advisers they dealt with frequently used the authority of their minister to overrule, ignore, and occasionally insult and bully permanent officials, with the predictable effect that many of them gave up on 'speaking truth to power': it was too intimidating, too costly, and too difficult to do so. If that is happening, it means that the civil service is not able to perform the role that, constitutionally, it is meant to: of providing impartial and objective advice on the democratically-elected government's policies. Wilkes himself stresses that 'vast swathes of policy happen – or are prevented – because of the work of spads'. He notes: 'The amount of formal and informal delegation to the special adviser raises another question: how can anyone tell whether they are exceeding their authority?' He adds that 'the straight answer is that they cannot'.[26]

You might ask why, if special advisers flout the spirit and the letter of their code in the way I have alleged, there are not many more reports of their misconduct. There are very few such reports. The Constitution Unit at University College London produced a research note that lists reports of misconduct by special advisers from 1997 to 2013. It reported that there had been 26 public allegations of misconduct by special advisers during that period, which works out at an average of less than two per year. But if I am correct, there are going to be numerous special advisers who violate the code routinely, probably every week and possibly every day. What explains the disparity between the way some of them behave and the absence of complaints about their conduct?

Public allegations of misconduct are those that reach the media, particularly newspapers. Newspapers are particularly interested in personal attacks conducted by special advisers on other ministers or members of the opposition, and in misconduct that involves special advisers dealing with the media. They are not generally interested in the workings of Whitehall. It was clearly a 'story' when Damian McBride, one of Gordon Brown's special advisers, was found to be planning to launch a website that would be devoted to personal attacks on political opponents. (In his book about his time as a special adviser, McBride also admits to planting in newspapers attacks on other Labour ministers, and to manufacturing a 'briefing war' which led to the sacking of Charles Clarke as home secretary.) It is difficult to see how a story entitled 'special adviser gives orders to civil servant' would ever make it into a national or even a provincial newspaper – so it is not surprising that none do. Furthermore, any permanent official who decided to go to a newspaper with claims that special advisers were violating the code by giving orders to civil servants would stand a very good chance of ending their career: a condition of their employment is not talking in public about the civil service. This is sufficient to explain why very few allegations of special adviser misconduct ever end up in the newspapers, and why those that are published almost invariably relate to allegations involving special advisers and their relations with the media.

Why, however, is there silence – as there seems to be – from permanent secretaries and other top civil servants on the matter? One reason may be that they are not often in a position to know what is happening. A permanent secretary of a large department usually does not observe the day to day interactions of special advisers and civil servants. Their job is to serve their minister. They know that special advisers are personally chosen by their minister, and have a closer relationship with him or her than does any permanent civil servant. They may simply not be aware of how special advisers are behaving towards mid-level or junior civil servants, and the way that it affects the work which those civil servants do.

Permanent secretaries may also be confused themselves about what special advisers are permitted to do. Sir Jonathan Stephens, who was permanent secretary at the Department for Culture, Media and Sport (DCMS) from 2006 to 2013, is a very experienced and well-regarded senior civil servant. Yet his interrogation before the Leveson Inquiry revealed that he was not aware that a special adviser should not take on the role of an intermediary in a quasi-judicial function – as Adam Smith, Jeremy Hunt's special adviser, appeared to do when Hunt, as culture secretary, had to consider whether to allow News Corporation's bid for BSkyB. Smith exchanged 500 texts, emails and phone conversations with an individual representing News International. News Corporation was then the holding company for News International, so providing information to that individual was effectively providing it to News Corporation.

The permanent secretary seems to have known about the contact and approved of it: Sir Jonathan stated that he was 'not aware of any guidance which suggests that it is inappropriate for special advisers to be involved in decisions of this sort',[27] a position which Lord Hart found 'astonishing'.[28] Lord Hart, a successful solicitor, had been expert legal adviser to the Labour lord chancellors Lord Irvine and Lord Falconer. On legal and constitutional matters, Lord Hart obviously knows what he is talking about. He thought it was obvious that special advisers should not be involved in that sort of decision, as did Charles Clarke, the former home secretary. Lord Hart's position is certainly the correct one: ministers or officials acting in a quasi-judicial capacity are expected to act impartially and apolitically. It would be rightly thought outrageous if any government decision on whether or not a takeover should be allowed was made on the basis of whether the company had done enough to help the party in power. Adam Smith's extensive contacts with a representative from News International made it look as if that is exactly how the decision was going to be taken. Moreover, the Code of Conduct for Special Advisers itself says that 'special advisers must not have any involvement in the award of external contracts'. In determining whether News Corporation could take over BSkyB, the DCMS was not strictly speaking awarding an external contract. But it was doing something very close to it. That is why Sir Jonathan's apparent inability to recognise that Smith was doing something wrong is so surprising.

Jeremy Hunt denied that he had authorised, or knew about, his special adviser's contact with News International. On the day that Adam Smith resigned, Sir

Jeremy Heywood, the cabinet secretary, wrote to all permanent secretaries to 'clarify the rigorous procedures that departments should have in place for handling all quasi-judicial decisions'. While the 'clarification' did not explicitly prohibit special advisers from being involved in those decisions, it emphasised:

> Quasi-judicial decisions are generally for the minister, with contacts normally made through official channels... There should be no private or favoured channels of communication with any one party... A special adviser approached by an interested party should refer the matter to the appropriate [civil service] official.[29]

If a civil servant of Sir Jonathan's standing and experience can fail to recognise a clear case of misconduct by a special adviser, it is hardly surprising that there is considerable confusion amongst all parties – ministers, civil servants, and special advisers – about what special advisers are actually permitted to do. And few cases of wrongdoing are going to be as blatant as Adam Smith's: because of the ambiguities in the Code of Conduct for Special Advisers, it is often going to be a matter of interpretation and of opinion as to whether what a special adviser has done counts as misconduct.

The code states:

> Where any permanent civil servant has concerns about any request coming from a special adviser, they should discuss that concern with their line manager, the special adviser concerned, the minister's principal private secretary or their permanent secretary. If a civil servant feels for whatever reason that he or she is unable to do this, then they may wish to raise the concern with the

> departmental nominated officer(s) or directly with
> the cabinet secretary or civil service commissioners.

That all sounds fine, but in practice, many civil servants told me that they felt extremely reluctant to take a step such as complaining about a special adviser's behaviour to a departmental nominated officer – let alone going to see the cabinet secretary or civil service commissioners.

The reason is not just that making complaints is seen as damaging to your career. It is also because, as Sir Jonathan Stephens found, it can be hard to be sure when a special adviser has done something wrong. The boundary between a 'request' and an order from a special adviser, for example, is not always obvious. It is frequently very unclear as to whether they have asked an official to do something that is the wrong side of the political boundary; or when they are deliberately suppressing or ignoring civil service advice in order to prevent the minister from being able to assess it. It is very difficult for civil servants to complain to the permanent secretary, or even to a line manager, when they are unsure of whether a line has been crossed and a special adviser has behaved in an improper or unacceptable way. The special adviser has the authority of the minister, and for many civil servants, talking to the special adviser will be the closest they ever get to providing the minister with advice.

The conduct of special advisers is anyway not the responsibility of the permanent secretary. It is the responsibility of the minister. The permanent secretary has no disciplinary, or even managerial, powers over special advisers. The 2010 Ministerial Code stresses that the ultimate responsibility for initiating any investigation into misconduct by a special adviser lies with the appointing minister. Everyone who works in the civil service is aware of the special relationship between special advisers and their minister, and how difficult and unwelcome it is to try to disturb or undermine it. Making an official complaint that special advisers are not treating civil servants correctly, or are failing to follow proper procedures, is a step that any junior or mid-ranking permanent official is very reluctant to take. Very few have done so, and the details of their complaints have not been made public, usually because the civil servant leaves with an out-of-court settlement, the condition of which is that neither side ever talks about it.

That ministers are responsible for disciplining their own special advisers in practice means that their code of behaviour depends on what their minister will let them get away with. Individual instances of unacceptable behaviour by special advisers often turn out to have been tacitly, and sometimes even explictly, endorsed by their ministers. Permanent secretaries rarely feel in a position to reprimand the minister they serve for giving too much leeway to a special adviser. As one retired senior civil servant, discussing the case of Jo Moore, told Yong and Hazell: 'Jo Moore wasn't under control because Byers [the secretary of state] did not want it. He gave her licence, she took it.'[30]

3

The new Machiavellis and the job of the court

There may be a further reason why permanent officials accept behaviour from special advisers that violates the code, and which they would not accept from other civil servants: they may recognise that, whilst civil servants are trained to be objective and impartial, and to be scrupulously honest in their dealings with the public, those qualities are not the ones most needed for political effectiveness – which civil servants obviously recognise is of primary importance to ministers, and is what special advisers are meant to help their minister achieve.

In an essay entitled 'Politics and Moral Character', the philosopher Bernard Williams argued that effectiveness in politics often requires some fairly unpleasant personal characteristics.[1] The argument goes back to Machiavelli – and in this context, it is significant that Jonathan Powell, Tony Blair's most powerful special adviser, entitled his book *The New Machiavelli*. That title signals very clearly that Powell thinks that, just as Machiavelli had shown many of the ethical principles that moralists ancient and medieval had thought should govern the conduct of princes were bogus and would lead to their ruin, so many procedures thought today by many authorities on government (such as, for example, senior civil servants) to be essential to good government are in fact pointless and only damage the ability of an elected government to wield power effectively.

For example, Machiavelli was unambiguous that princes should only tell the truth when it was to their advantage – and since there were plenty of occasions when it would be more expedient to lie, a sensible prince would lie frequently. This was shocking in the 16th century, and it is shocking now: as citizens, we expect to be told the truth by our rulers. For an elected politician, especially one wielding executive power, to be caught lying to parliament or indeed in any public statement is a resigning offence. The obligation to tell the truth is usually thought to run to all government officials. It would certainly be thought outrageous if any official document stated that a certain class of officials were excused from the obligation to tell the truth to the public, in the way that special advisers are excused from the civil service requirement to be impartial and objective. Honesty is one of the fundamental principles of government service in a democracy – and the Code of Conduct for Special Advisers duly states that 'special advisers should not deceive or knowingly mislead the public'.

Jonathan Powell, however, seems to agree with Machiavelli that an absolute prohibition on lying to the public is unreasonable, and is one that special advisers should not take too seriously. *In The New Machiavelli*, he states, for example:

> A leader must be seen in public to be a superman, although of course he is an ordinary mortal like everyone else. It is the job of the court [i.e., the staff at Number 10] to make him appear other than he

really is... A prime minister is therefore never allowed to be sick.[2]

Powell seems to be claiming that politically effective officials should deliberately deceive the public on the state of the leader's health. Covering up Tony Blair's physical ailments, as Powell stresses that he and his team did, may seem trivial, and in many ways it is, but it is the thin end of a very thick wedge. An official prepared to lie about a trivial matter is more likely to be prepared to lie about a serious one – which is why there is a carefully incubated culture within the civil service of telling the truth about everything, even minor matters.[3]

This is not to say that permanent civil servants have never been known to mislead the public. Obviously they have done so, and no doubt some of them still do. It is simply to point out that the culture of the civil service is strongly against it – in a way that, if Jonathan Powell is correct, the culture of special advisers is not, and should not be. Once again, the argument is falsified if made into an all-or-nothing proposition, with inflexibly honest civil servants on one side, and relentlessly mendacious special advisers on the other. That extreme position does not accurately describe what happens, and it is no part of my argument that it should. My claim is rather that special advisers are more likely to subordinate the principles that civil servants think should dictate their actions – such as honesty and integrity – to considerations of political effectiveness, with the results that Machiavelli would have thought entirely appropriate.

In 1986 Lord (Robert) Armstrong, then cabinet secretary, admitted under cross examination in a courtroom in Australia that he had been 'economical with the truth' in one of his letters: he had suggested in correspondence with the publishers of Peter Wright's *Spycatcher* that Whitehall officials had not read the book, when in fact some had. His misleading statement – he insisted that's what it was, rather than an outright lie – was on a trivial matter, and one irrelevant to the government's case. But it generated an enormous amount of odium. Armstrong himself never accepted that he had been culpably dishonest. He shared the almost universal sentiment that it was quite wrong that a civil servant, especially one of the most senior in Britain, should tell less than the whole truth on any matter. That is still the position within the civil service: telling the truth is a central value, and it should never be compromised, certainly not for the aim of securing party political advantage.

As a special adviser, Jonathan Powell may possibly have had a less rigid attitude to truth-telling. Let's grant that he and Machiavelli are right that effective political action requires not being too scrupulous about keeping to conventional moral rules, such as always telling the truth. But as citizens in a democracy – as opposed to members of a political party seeking party political advantages – we have an interest in not being lied to on any matter by government officials. That is why most of us are relieved that the culture of truth-telling has been so carefully inculcated in the civil service, and are eager that it should remain.

Civil servants, however, may themselves recognise that there is something in Machiavelli's (and Powell's) claim that political effectiveness requires a willingness to depart from a strict adherence to principles such as always telling the truth to the public – and that recognition may restrict their ability to object when special advisers do such things which they, as permanent civil servants, are trained to take care *not* to do: such as issuing misleading statements or giving politically slanted assessments of the impact of particular policy proposals. Civil servants may be able to keep their integrity intact, and their commitment to honesty, impartiality and objectivity unimpugned, by leaving special advisers to do the 'dirty work' necessary for political effectiveness. But the cost is that special advisers' role increases in significance, and civil service advice is marginalised to an ever-increasing degree.

It takes a certain degree of confidence for a civil servant to advise their minister that the policy they have been elected to implement is mistaken, and to state: 'No minister. This policy is a waste of money: it will not work.' There is a recognised procedure which a permanent secretary – who is constitutionally responsible for accounting to parliament's Public Accounts Committee on how money in the department in which he or she works is spent – can follow should they be convinced, after considering the evidence, that pursuing a particular policy or action to which the minister is attached would be a waste of public money, or in some way improper or illegal. Permanent secretaries can insist that they will not implement the policy without a 'ministerial direction': written instructions from the minister. When that happens, the minister, not the permanent secretary, now becomes personally responsible for justifying to parliament how the money will be spent. That procedure usually forces a ministerial reconsideration of the policy. Still, if having reconsidered it the minister continues to think that the policy is worth its cost, he is entitled to overrule the permanent secretary, and the permanent secretary is obliged to implement it.

Lord (Gus) O'Donnell, the former cabinet secretary, described a permanent secretary's decision to ask for a ministerial direction as 'the nuclear option'. It is not used very often: there have been fewer than 55 ministerial directions issued in the 25 years since 1990.[4] Issuing a request for a ministerial direction usually indicates a breakdown of some kind in the relationship between the permanent secretary and the minister. A fundamental disagreement on whether a policy counts as value for money or complies with legality or propriety cannot happen without a very significant loss of trust.

It is hard to work out whether there have been more requests for ministerial directions issued in the last decade than in earlier periods, because until 2011, neither the fact that a ministerial direction had been issued, nor its content, was made public with any regularity. It is even harder to work out what it would mean if there had been an increase in requests for ministerial directions: would it mean that the relationship between ministers and permanent secretaries was breaking down more often? Or would it mean that permanent secretaries had more confidence in opposing their minister's wishes? It is difficult to know for sure, but it is unlikely to mean that permanent secretaries have more confidence in opposing ministerial wishes today than they used to. There is a consensus that – as Bernard Jenkin, the chairman of the Public Administration Select Committee, put it – 'ever since the time of Margaret Thatcher, when she started to try to change the civil service, there is the sense that the civil service no longer has the confidence to tell the truth to power in the way that it did'.[5]

Because she was such a forceful and energetic politician, and because she expressed her convictions so directly, Mrs Thatcher's scepticism about the reliability and effectiveness of the civil service had a very powerful effect. She made no secret of the fact that she thought that civil servants were timid, risk averse, and reconciled to managing Britain's national decline. She wanted to reduce their pay and pensions. Sir John Hoskyns, who was head of her policy unit at Number 10 until May 1982, insisted that her priority was to 'deprivilege the civil service'. She brought in Sir Derek Rayner, the former boss of Marks and Spencer, to shake it up. She abolished the Central Policy Review Staff (CPRS), an organisation half of whose staff consisted of career civil servants, and whose purpose was to suggest policy initiatives that would help to deal with changes over the long term. That move was described by Sir Ian Bancroft, then head of the civil service, as a 'sad blow by prejudice against civilisation.' He retired early, two and a half years after she was first elected. The CPRS's role was taken over by the policy unit, which had a significantly higher portion of its staff chosen for their political commitments.[6]

But although her rhetoric was extremely critical of the civil service, Mrs Thatcher in fact drew on the advice of senior civil servants to a considerable extent. She worked very closely with the officials she trusted, such as Robert Armstrong, Robin Butler and Charles Powell. The longer she was in Number 10, the more she seemed to appreciate the institution's virtues. By the time she wrote her autobiography, she could state: 'The sheer professionalism of the British civil service, which allows governments to come and go with a minimum of dislocation and a maximum of efficiency, is something other countries with different systems have every cause to envy.'[7] By the standards of Tony Blair, Gordon Brown and David Cameron, she had very few outside advisers providing an alternative to senior civil servants' counsel: she only appointed 14 special and expert advisers over the whole period of her premiership, compared with the more than a hundred outside advisers that Blair, Brown and Cameron have each had working for them. All the same, her hostile pronouncements in public about the civil service unquestionably helped legitimise the view that a government that was determined to get things done efficiently and quickly needed to bypass senior civil servants by bringing in energetic and above all politically committed outsiders who could be relied upon to implement policies, rather than to criticise them.

When Tony Blair became prime minister in 1997, he arrived with 73 special advisers. He and his cabinet took it for granted that the civil service could not be trusted to give impartial and objective advice: the views of civil servants, probably Conservative to begin with, were bound to have been shaped by 15 years of serving the Tories. Patrick Diamond, an adviser to Blair, wrote in an article for *Political Studies Review* in 2011 that 'civil servants were often treated as an accident waiting to happen, and were thought [by the Blair government] largely incapable of producing rigorous, evidence-based policy'. Jonathan Powell, Blair's chief of staff, claimed that when it came to assessing how well any individual minister was doing, 'ministers' drivers usually had a far better [that is, more accurate] assessment of them than their permanent secretaries.' Gordon Brown was notorious for not trusting most of his civil service officials, preferring to 'work almost exclusively through an inner group of loyal advisers'.[8]

Tony Blair's own attitude towards the civil service appeared to have moderated by 2004. After nearly seven years in government, he gave a speech on civil service reform which started by praising civil servants. He insisted: 'The myth on which young Labour activists were reared in the 1970s and 80s of a civil service that was Tory to its bones, turned out to be just that: a myth.' He emphasised that the civil service 'has strengths that are priceless. The greatest is indeed its integrity.' But he also stressed: 'The principal challenge [that the civil service has to face] is to shift from policy advice to delivery.' He made it clear that while he recognised and appreciated the civil service's ability to give advice 'without fear or favour', he didn't want it. What he needed from the civil service was not advice, but the efficient and effective implementation of the policies that he and his special advisers had already decided on. And his main complaint, and the main reason why he thought the civil service needed reform, was that it was not performing that executive function properly. It was still trying to mould policy – a role he thought was no longer appropriate for the civil service 'in the modern world'. As part of switching senior civil servants from being policy advisers to project managers, he proposed a four-year limit on all senior posts, and to make it much easier to appoint outsiders to top civil service positions. So while Blair appeared to be celebrating the structure built by Northcote and Trevelyan - which has the civil service working as a junior partner with the elected government in producing workable and effective policy – he was in fact undermining it.[9]

The process of changing the civil service from being a source of independent policy advice into an agency that implements government policy, but does not help to make it, continued during the Conservative and Liberal Democrat Coalition. Although the Coalition Agreement promised that the new government would 'put a limit on the number of special advisers', which suggested their number would be reduced, David Cameron has in fact increased them: well over 100 were employed by the Coalition. The prime minister has 26 special advisers working just for him. Cameron promised to give the civil service back its role in policy advice. But the claim that the Downing Street Policy Unit was 'entirely staffed by civil servants' was misleading, since it suggested that the organisation was staffed by career civil servants, politically independent individuals committed to the impartial and objective assessment of policy. But many of them were political appointees on short-term contracts, chosen at least partly because of the strength of their political convictions. Officially, special advisers are misleadingly categorised as 'civil servants', albeit temporary ones.[10] As prime minister, David Cameron turned out to be rather less keen on policy advice from civil service officials committed to the Northcote-Trevelyan values of impartiality and objectivity than his statements as leader of the opposition suggested.

That the government should take advice from people who are not career civil servants is not necessarily a bad thing – most career civil servants think it is a good idea that ministers should have sources of advice other than career civil servants. The issue is not the *fact* of outside, politically committed advice, but the *extent* to which it has come to dominate, and to replace, the objective and impartial advice provided by civil servants.

Put aside for a moment the question of whether the attempt to switch the focus of the civil service from policy advice to 'delivery' has made for better or worse government: the issue here is the effect on the morale of civil service officials of that switch, together with the arrival of large numbers of special advisers, many of whom believe that their access to the secretary of state gives them authority to direct civil servants. There cannot be much doubt that the principal effect has been to accelerate their loss of self-confidence. Professors Anthony King and Ivor Crewe conclude:

> Our study of blunders suggests that officials have become reluctant to speak truth to power. They do not want to speak largely because they believe power does not want to listen. Objection is construed as obstruction. Again and again in our interviews, former ministers as well as retired civil servants commented that even when officials had harboured serious reservations about ministers' latest bright ideas, they failed openly to express their reservations.[11]

In theory, one of the great advantages of a permanent civil service is that it is the repository of a 'corporate memory': officials who have been in the same department for several years should have a sense of what works and what does not, because they have seen the effects of several different governments' policies.[12] It is not necessarily a feature that is always appreciated by ministers in a hurry to implement what they believe to be new, innovative policies. As Jonathan Powell says:

> This deeply engrained fatalism is a serious problem in the upper reaches of the civil service. Having been a civil servant myself, it is easy to understand how it develops. When you have been wrestling with a problem for decades and you are familiar with how difficult it is to resolve, when you know there are no easy answers and are reconciled to failing again and again, it is difficult not to be cynical about the fresh-eyed, bushy-tailed

aspirations of a new minister who knows next to nothing about the problem and whose 'new' policies are not new at all... From a minister's point of view, [civil servants'] negativism can become tiresome. He looks for a can-do spirit which instead of incessantly pointing out the difficulties will come up with solutions.[13]

Francis Maude made essentially the same point in his evidence to PASC in 2012, when explaining why senior civil servants are not as effective at implementing policies as ministers want them to be:

Some of it is the old thing of 'ministers come and ministers go. We are the permanent civil service. We have been here, and our forebears have been here, for 150 years, and the system will exist after ministers go'.[14]

Corporate memory has unquestionably very seriously declined within many departments in the last two decades. That decline has coincided with the rise of special advisers. It may be a coincidence rather than cause and effect. But the extent of the decline is certainly striking.

Part of the explanation is that there is a very high turnover of officials. Senior civil servants do not stay as long in any one department as they used to. This means that they do not build up a repository of knowledge and experience – or if they do, they move on just as they start to be in a position to be able to put it to use. Between 2010 and 2012, all but two of the permanent secretaries in 16 government departments changed. In four departments, there were three different permanent secretaries in two years. The former Labour minister Lord (Andrew) Adonis observed: 'It is a misnomer to describe what we have as a permanent civil service. It is an impermanent civil service... it lacks the key attributes of continuity and expertise.'[15] Christopher Hood, Gladstone Professor of Government at Oxford University, testified that when he 'did a study in the 1990s of a civil service organisation, [it] had a 40 per cent turnover a year, and as a result, it had virtually no corporate memory; it could not even remember things that had happened three months before, and it had to spend its whole time in meetings socialising people to what had been happening.'[16]

Another cause of the loss of corporate memory is the move to electronic documents. Almost all reports, and all items of official communication, are now written on computers. There seems to be no system for filing documents generated on a computer in a way that means they can be easily accessed by officials eager to know what was said in the past on a particular topic. Many special advisers do not think this is a problem, for the reason that Jonathan Powell expresses: consulting civil servants' past reflections will only reveal problems, when what is needed are solutions.

In a minor way, I had, during my spell at the Home Office, direct experience of the difficulties the inability to access what has been done in the past can cause. One of Theresa May's special advisers told me that the home secretary wanted to give a statement to parliament on the police's use of the technique known as stop and search. Part of the motive for doing this, he explained, was political: stop and search is a policy which consistently alienates members of the black community. I was told that it would help the home secretary's standing with Afro-Caribbeans if she made a statement that was critical of the police's use of stop and search.

The grounds would essentially be that the tool was racist, or at least used by the police in a racist way: the statistics demonstrated that you were six or seven times more likely to be stopped and searched if you were a member of an ethnic minority.

In fact, the Home Office had done research in the relatively recent past which showed that the statistics do not demonstrate this. P.A.J. Waddington, now a professor at Wolverhampton University, worked for the Home Office during the late 1990s and the early years of this century. In the wake of the publication of the Macpherson report into the Metropolitan Police investigation into the murder of Stephen Lawrence, Waddington was part of a Home Office team that looked carefully at the Met's use of stop and search. The task was to establish if indeed it was being used in a racist way, as the 'six or seven times more likely' statistic suggests. It was noted that the statistic was obtained by looking at the percentage of the total number of stop and search incidents that a particular ethnic group was subject to, and then dividing it by the percentage that that ethnic group makes up of the population of the UK as a whole. If you then compare the figure that calculation generates for whites with the figure you get for ethnic minorities, the result is that members of ethnic minorities are 'six or seven times more likely to be stopped' than white people.

The Home Office research showed that calculating relative stop and search rates in that way is very misleading. If you want to know if the police are stopping and searching members of particular ethnic groups in a biased and possibly racist way, then what you need to know is who is available to be stopped and searched on the streets at the times that the police are stopping and searching people. For instance, the police stop and search a miniscule number of women, of all races, over the age of 70. Does this show they are biased in favour of these women? Obviously not. It simply shows that the police do not receive reports that women over the age of 70 have been involved in mugging people on the streets – and therefore they are not useful or appropriate targets for being stopped and searched. Women over the age of 70 also tend not to be on the streets at the times and in the places the police do stop and search.

The team of Home Office researchers felt it was important to know the ethnic composition of the population available to be stopped and searched in the places and at the times the police were implementing that tactic. So they went out and counted it: they identified the percentage of the street population made up by each ethnic group. They then compared that with the percentage of stop and searches that were made up by each ethnic group. They discovered that, when you looked at who was available to be stopped and searched when the police were actually stopping and searching on the streets, the ethnic bias disappeared. In fact, the police stopped slightly more white people than they should have done if you looked solely at their proportion of the street population. The police, the Home Office research showed, did not target particular areas for stop and search because they wanted to stop and search people of a particular ethnic group. They chose those areas because that's where the highest amount of street crime was reported – and stop and search's primary purpose is to diminish street crimes such as mugging and robbery.[17]

But a decade later, not one official within the Home Office seemed aware of this work. No-one had heard of it. No-one could tell me where I could find it. There was no Home Office library where such items were catalogued and so available for being accessed – or if there was, no official I talked to knew about it. I nevertheless felt that it was important that this truth be reflected in any parliamentary statement made by the home secretary. It would certainly be possible to point out that there are many things wrong with stop and search, because there are: it is often implemented badly; those stopped are not given adequate reasons *why* they are being stopped; they are often treated rudely and without the respect they are entitled to. But on its own, the statistical evidence of the way it is used does not suggest that it is implemented in a racist way.

So that is what I put in my draft of her parliamentary statement. The reaction was an explosion of rage from the special adviser, and an emphatic assertion that Waddington's point - that statistics on stop and search do not support the idea that it is implemented by the police in a racist way – would not be in the speech. He told me: 'Of course I could take this up with the home secretary.' But he did not. I doubt she was ever informed that the statistic used to demonstrate police race bias in the application of stop and search was misleading. The special adviser re-wrote the statement in the way he wanted it, with the misleading statistic, and she gave the statement to parliament as he had written it on 2 July 2013. The misleading statistic has reappeared in the home secretary's subsequent statements to parliament on the topic (see, for example, her statement on 30 April 2014).

It is worth emphasising that the Home Office had no corporate memory of research commissioned only a decade previously. It had no repository for that research. If this experience is representative, then it is no wonder that some of the same policy mistakes get repeated time after time: there is no facility that enables anyone to learn from the past. To avoid making the same mistakes as your predecessors, you first have to know what those mistakes were.

4

The patronage virus and incompetent government

It is rare to find anyone who will come out and state bluntly we would be better governed without the benefit of a civil service dedicated to giving ministers the benefit of the impartial and objective assessment of their policies. As I have already mentioned, nearly everyone, including ministers, stresses that they are in favour of that. There are, however, several politicians who have said that they think the appointment of the most senior officials in the civil service should be on the basis of political patronage: they should be short-term appointments chosen by the secretary of state.

Francis Maude's proposals in the Civil Service Reform Plan of 2012, which would mean that ministers were able to appoint their own permanent secretaries, appear to aim at ensuring that permanent secretaries were politically committed to implementing the secretary of state's policies – although he denied that was what he wanted. But the Lords Constitution Committee, which investigated Maude's proposals, concluded: 'Temporary civil servants appointed in this [Maude's] manner may not feel able to speak truth unto power, particularly if there is an expectation that temporary appointments may be extended or made permanent at the conclusion of the fixed term. There is a risk that such appointments may be used as a means of increasing the political element of the civil service by the back door, or lead to cronyism.'[1]

At the time of writing (September 2015), those proposals have not yet been formally adopted by the present Conservative government.[2] But there is a good chance that they will be. While Francis Maude is no longer an MP, David Cameron supported and endorsed his plans for the reform of the civil service, including his plans to give secretaries of state a much bigger role in the way that their permanent secretaries are appointed. Although the Conservative manifesto for the 2015 General Election stated that the Conservatives 'value our outstanding public servants' and that 'Britain's impartial, professional and highly capable civil service is admired around the world and one of our nation's strengths', there is no indication that the prime minister has altered his views on the need to change the way permanent secretaries are appointed so as to make them more responsive to the secretary of state's political priorities.

Furthermore, David Cameron, when prime minister of the Coalition government, endorsed 'extended ministerial offices' (EMOs), a proposal which allows a secretary of state to expand their private office by employing additional advisers from outside the civil service. There is no formal limit on the number of additional advisers, but they have to be funded within existing budgets and approved by the prime minister. There are various restrictions imposed on what they are supposed to do, which include a prohibition on giving explicitly political advice. Perhaps those restrictions will be adhered to. It seems more likely, however, that they will be as closely observed as the ones that are supposed to prevent special advisers from giving instructions to civil servants.

Prior to the 2015 election, no secretary of state took up the opportunity to employ more advisers from outside the civil service, perhaps because there seemed not much point in doing so: little departmental business is done during the run-up to a general election. But since the Conservatives' victory in May 2015, several ministers have said that they will do it, including Nicky Morgan, secretary of state for education, who wants to appoint five additional advisers from outside the civil service, and Amber Rudd, secretary of state for energy.

EMOs mark a further step in diminishing the role played by civil servants in providing advice. Their primary role will not be to evaluate objectively and impartially the policies that the secretary of state has arrived in office to implement. It will be to endorse and to implement whatever has already been decided. They will aim to protect the secretary of state from criticism, not to expose him or her to it. It is already very difficult for all but the most senior civil servants even to put a proposal to a minister which has not been vetted first by political advisers. Extended ministerial offices are likely to make it impossible.[3]

The gradual replacement of advice from impartial permanent officials by counsel from politically committed advisers suggests, once again, that many ministers' repeated statements that they are dedicated to preserving an objective, impartial civil service appointed solely on merit are not quite what they seem. In theory, elected politicians may be able to see that it makes for good government if policies are subjected to objective and impartial scrutiny, and that they should be implemented by people who do not let party political considerations interfere with their decisions – especially when a political party other than their own is in power.

In practice, however, when holding the reins of government, and trying to keep their promises to the electorate and get the policies in their manifesto implemented quickly and effectively, they demonstrate a marked lack of enthusiasm for the process of impartial and objective advice, preferring the enthusiasm and commitment of politically committed special advisers who have been selected not on the basis of open competition, but through ministerial patronage. If that process continues – and I emphasise again that it is a process, not something controlled by an on/off switch – then we will eventually end up with policies being implemented, and executive power being exercised, without the benefit of *any* impartial, objective advice. There will be no counterweight to the power of people whose most pressing concern is to further the interests of the political party that they serve.

There are many reasons for thinking that this development will not improve the chances of good government, and that, as citizens and taxpayers, we should be hostile to any changes that will end up by making it pervasive. The impartial scrutiny of policy significantly diminishes the chances that governments will make laws and implement procedures that are wasteful and impractical – but which benefit the politicians who support them. It is easier than many people seem to realise to squander our inheritance of relatively efficient and uncorrupt government, and replace it with what is the default position of most states: government based on political patronage.

The appointment of senior civil servants strictly on merit, and their ability to give objective and impartial advice, are not the same thing. But the two go together. Officials who are explicitly politically committed are not going to be objective and impartial in their assessments of their own party's policies. It was the awareness of that truth that persuaded Northcote and Trevelyan in 1854 that if Britain was to be well-governed, it needed a class of permanent officials who were not aligned to any political party, and who were appointed solely on the basis of their ability to perform their service to the government in an efficient and effective way.

Northcote and Trevelyan were right that one of the purposes of the civil service is to reduce the chances that unreasonable convictions would get in the way of effective administration. It is to act as a check on the attempt to implement proposals that could not succeed because they have been inadequately thought through and are not going to achieve their intended result; or which should not be allowed to do so, because they were an attempt to do things which no government should attempt to do (such as – to take two contemporary examples – to qualify the prohibition on imprisonment without a prior fair trial so as to permit the indefinite detention of foreign nationals accused of terrorist offences, or to authorise the use of torture by state agents).

That is why they thought that:

> ...the government of the country could not be carried on without the aid of an efficient body of permanent officers... possessing sufficient independence, character, ability and experience to be able to advise, assist, and to some extent, to influence those who are from time to time set over them.

These people would be servants of the Crown, the symbol of permanent government and authority, rather than of any party that happened to be in office. This was the origin of the idea that civil servants should 'speak truth unto power'. Their role was not simply to do whatever they were told to; it was to point out to ministers when their proposals were unworkable, impractical, illegal or unethical, and to advise them against attempting to implement such plans – and thereby to prevent, or at least to delay, their implementation. They should also suggest alternatives that would be free of the defects they identified.

No-one should think that the return of a patronage system in this country, with all its negative effects on the integrity and efficiency of government, is impossible. 'The patronage virus is never dead', observed the former cabinet secretary Lord (Richard) Wilson, evidently drawing on his own experience at the heart of government, 'and constantly needs to be beaten back'. The evidence from the history of government in both Britain and other countries suggests Lord Wilson's statement is correct.

Still, the emphasis on the importance of advice from impartial and objective officials appointed on merit may nevertheless seem fundamentally mistaken, on the grounds that it violates democratic principles. When the Northcote-Trevelyan reforms were first projected, Britain was not a full democracy, and it would not be one even when those reforms had been (mostly) implemented by the start of the First World War: women did not have the vote, and nor did men who were unable to meet the property qualification. Today, there is universal suffrage in this country. Ministers belong to and have been chosen by the party that has received endorsement by election. Civil servants, however, have not been endorsed by any form of democratic vote. They therefore cannot claim any right to independent political power. What legitimate power they may possess, they possess because ministers delegate it to them, on the understanding that they will carry out the instructions issued to them. Ministers can take that power back whenever they wish to – and they should take it back whenever any official does not do what they have been instructed to.

So what can possibly be wrong with giving ministers complete authority to select who serves them? How can the marginalisation of advice from non-politically aligned officials be seen as anything other than the legitimate extension of democratic authority – the only legitimate authority that there is? That argument is put by Michael Jacobs, who is visiting professor in the Department of Politics/School of Public Policy at University College London, and was a special adviser to Gordon Brown between 2004 and 2010: 'It is not clear why career officials – who are unelected and unaccountable – should have greater legitimacy to guide the policy process than advisers... advisers get their mandate from, and are accountable to, the elected minister. In this sense, political advisers could arguably be said to have greater legitimacy than officials in presenting choices to ministers.'[5]

The point can be pressed further. In a democracy, all legitimate authority derives ultimately from the consent of those over whom that power is exercised. 'Consent' is interpreted broadly, as it has to be for it to be possible to govern any state whose population is less than totally unanimous on every political and ethical issue. Those who did not vote for the winning party are assumed nonetheless to consent to be ruled by the democratic system: we are all taken to accept that the winners of free and fair elections are entitled to form the legitimate government. It means that ministers can claim that when they exercise political power, they exercise it with the consent of all the people, and not just those who voted for them. Civil servants cannot say this. No-one voted for them at all. And that is why they cannot claim to exercise legitimate political power in their own right.

Is there anything wrong with this argument? It is certainly correct to maintain that all legitimate political authority derives from consent, broadly conceived. It is also correct that under our constitution, a majority in the House of Commons, usually formed by the political party that the majority represents, is taken to have the consent of the electorate; and that consent is presumed to extend to all of the policies that are endorsed by the government formed from that majority. But does it follow from this that any check on policies supported by a duly-elected government must be illegitimate? It does not. It is universally recognised that democratically-elected governments can want to implement policies that are wasteful, ineffective, oppressive, unethical or just plain stupid. If the argument that there can be no legitimate check on policies endorsed by the majority were correct, then it would be a kind of category mistake to criticise a policy that a democratically-elected government wished to implement: that the policy had the support of the majority would guarantee that it was right.

But of course the fact that a policy has been endorsed by the majority does not mean that it is impossible to find faults with it and to question whether it is the right thing to do. All mature democracies have devised some way of placing checks on what one of the framers of the American Constitution, James Madison, called the propensity of elected governments for 'wicked or improper projects' – a phrase which, by the logic of the 'democratic' argument, should be an oxymoron. There is no contradiction in the idea that in a democracy, while the government elected by the majority of the people is and ought to be sovereign, there should nevertheless be some restraints on what the elected government can do with its power. Furthermore, were the argument that there should be no such restraints correct, it would follow that it would not merely be legitimate, but morally necessary, to politicise all institutions that exercise any political power whatever, where 'politicise' means 'make them accord completely with the will of the party which won the last election'. That would be the only way to ensure that every political institution reflected the consent of the people, and so was in a position to wield power legitimately.

In Britain, there are in fact several institutions with legitimate authority whose purpose is to act as a check on the will of the majority. They are not supposed to thwart it, and ultimately, if the majority in the House of Commons decides to overrule their objections, it is entitled to do so. The institutions nevertheless exist in order to ensure that the majority does not have completely unrestricted power: their purpose is to restrain the elected government's occasional propensity to do unreasonable, unethical or otherwise inadvisable things. The House of Lords is one example of such an institution. Its purpose at present is to scrutinise and to sometimes to delay legislation passed by the Commons, with the object of persuading the Commons to revise its proposals in the way the Lords think is appropriate. The

Lords cannot overturn legislation passed by a majority in the Commons. They can only require the Commons to 'think again'. If, having thought again, the Commons is still determined to implement the policy the Lords oppose, there is nothing further the Lords can do about it. But it is widely, if not universally, recognised that it is sensible to have, as part of the process of law-making, a procedure which can require the government to pause and re-assess its own proposals before imposing them as law.

The judiciary is another institution which, within certain specified limits, is entitled to act as a restraint on policies that have been endorsed by the elected government. Historically, judges have been able to ask the government to review a law, and even to quash it, on the basis that it violates a principle of natural justice (such as the right to a fair hearing, or the right not to be judged by someone who has a personal stake in the outcome of the case), or is so irrational that no reasonable person could possibly endorse it. Since the incorporation of the European Convention of Human Rights into British law, the judges on the Supreme Court have also been able to declare that a piece of legislation is incompatible with the rights specified in the convention. None of this gives judges the power to overturn a policy to which the elected government is committed. Parliament can always pass another law (as, for example, happened when the Appeal Court ruled that the government had been wrong to spend development money on helping Malaysia construct the Pergau Dam[6]). But by ruling that a policy is incompatible with the Human Rights Act, senior judges can increase the political costs of pursuing it very considerably, to the point where the elected government decides that modifying or abandoning the initial law is the better alternative. That has been the outcome on every occasion when the Supreme Court has issued such a ruling, as it did in the case of the Blair government's policy of indefinite detention of terrorist suspects without trial.

Both the House of Lords and the Supreme Court lack democratic legitimacy, in the straightforward sense that neither judges nor the members of the Lords are elected, and they are not directly 'accountable to the people'. Their decisions are frequently criticised on that basis, particularly by politicians whose policies they delay or declare to be in some way illegitimate. Nonetheless, I don't think there is any politician of any major political party who would say that the whole idea that there should be checks on the kinds of laws a democratically-elected legislature can enact is just *wrong*. The argument is about how extensive those checks should be, what form they should take, and how they should be implemented. It is not about whether they should be there at all. It is perfectly compatible with commitment to democracy to believe that within the government, there should be a body of impartial and objective officials, selected according to their ability rather than on the basis of political patronage, whose purpose is to scrutinise government policies and to advise ministers on whatever short-comings those policies may have. That is the role of the civil service – or at least it has been.

Should we, as taxpayers and citizens, want policies which the government has been elected to implement to be scrutinised objectively and impartially before they are made into law? I do not see how that question can reasonably be answered with anything other than 'yes' – even though objective and impartial scrutiny does not infallibly identify 'wicked or improper projects' (and even if it did, officials would not be in a position to prevent ministers from going ahead with them). In many cases, officials will fail to recognise potential problems or be unable to articulate them clearly. They may also invent problems that are not actually there. But it must be the case that such scrutiny will reduce the likelihood of policy blunders, at least compared with the situation in which there is none, and the closest policies get to impartial scrutiny is the enthusiastic endorsement of politically committed supporters.

As far as I know, no-one has attempted to assess the extent to which civil service advice has prevented ministers from implementing policies that, had they been put into practice, would have had disastrous consequences. Like most historical hypotheticals, it is something that is more or less impossible to assess, because it is impossible to know with any certainty what *would* have happened had policies that were abandoned or modified been implemented in their original form. But permanent officials obviously fail fairly often to persuade ministers to modify bad policy ideas, because there has been plenty of bad policy since the Second World War, much of which has had effects opposite to those intended. The closest I know to an audit of government policy successes and failures is *Blunders of Our Governments*, by Anthony King and Ivor Crewe. Professor Crewe concludes from his part in that study:

> Misgovernment is more often the result of over-hasty and ideologically-driven ministers ignoring the advice of their officials and outside experts, and pressing ahead with proposals in a highly centralised system of government that lacks checks and balances.[6]

It is easier to identify examples of policies that senior civil servants *should* have intervened to try to prevent ministers from pressing ahead with – but did not. Professors King and Crewe list many in *Blunders of Our Governments*, including the poll tax, the Child Support Agency, the NHS IT system, the system of regional fire control centres and the system of tax credits introduced by Gordon Brown. Margaret Hodge, the Labour MP who was chair of the Public Accounts Committee for the 2010-2015 parliament, adds the decision of the last Labour government to enter a contract for the purchase of two aircraft carriers when the money to pay for them was not available – which led to delays that added an estimated £2 billion to the cost.[8] It may be too early to identify clear policy blunders committed by ministers in the Coalition government that lasted from 2010 to 2015. But Professors King and Crewe are of the view that we can be sure there have been many.

There would, however, almost certainly have been more of them had there *only* been politically committed advisers, and no impartial officials. Despite the failures to prevent incompetent policies catalogued in *Blunders of Our Governments*, it is better for the government of this country that we should, as Northcote and Trevelyan proposed, have 'permanent officers... possessing sufficient independence, character, ability and experience to be able to advise, assist, and to some extent, to influence those who are from time to time set over them.' Their political independence is essential to their value. Otherwise, it is just a case of 'buying several copies of the morning newspaper in order to assure yourself that what it said was true'.[9]

None of this implies that permanent officials all perform their role perfectly, or that the civil service is not in need of reform. There are clearly problems inherent in an order of bureaucrats who spend all of their careers in the service of the state. Officials are often not objective and impartial in the way that they should be. They can be captured by special interest groups. They can treat compliance with arcane procedure as if it were an inflexible moral code. They can succumb to inertia, and elevate the avoidance of any risk to ludicrous heights. But in this context, the most significant question is: do those problems pose a greater threat to the possibility of efficient and uncorrupt government than the alternative?

At the moment, the alternative is to hire, on short-term contracts, either politically committed people, or businessmen who have demonstrated great success in the private sector – let us call it 'the market'. I think I have sufficiently outlined the threat that politically committed advisers can pose to efficient and uncorrupt government. There are examples of civil servants who, once they become special advisers, can lie and cheat with as great abandon as anyone: Damian McBride, the Labour special adviser who admitted fabricating stories in an effort to discredit Gordon Brown's political rivals, is a notorious example. But examples of McBride's kind only illustrate that an organisation which aims to bequeath to its members the values of integrity and honesty sometimes fails to do so. They do not show that it always fails, or that it has less success in passing those values on than firms that do not even try. Generally, people who spend long periods as career civil servants *do* internalise the values of impartiality, honesty, integrity and objectivity, and to a remarkable extent.

Is there any reason to think that people who have been raised in the ethos, not of the civil service, but of the market, will have the commitment to integrity, honesty, objectivity and impartiality that should characterise government service? The behaviour of executives of companies operating in the market such as banks, for example, is not encouraging. To judge from the amount of mis-selling of financial products, many of them appear to have regarded the ignorance of their customers as a resource to be exploited. Bank executives have important virtues, including energy, dynamism, managerial ability, entrepreneurial skill and openness to new ideas. But honesty, integrity and impartiality often do not appear to be among them.

Conclusion

Keeping our government straight

Politicians who have access to the levers of the state's power are faced with the perennial temptations of using their power to further their own interests or the interests of their supporters rather than those of the people as a whole. Democratic politicians face this temptation just as much as the tyrants who have seized power by force or fraud and keep it by using those methods. Democratically-elected politicians know that their hold on power depends on persuading the electorate that their policies are bringing about success and prosperity, combined with justice, individual liberty, and not too great a degree of inequality. The constant temptation is to pretend that things are going better than they really are: to convince the public that all is well, that policies are having the results they intended, and that if anything has gone wrong, it is the fault of the last lot. Truth-telling about the effects of the use of political power is essential to the proper working of democracy. But politicians in power are constantly tempted not to tell the truth.

That is perhaps the most fundamental reason why officials who are politically independent, and who are dedicated to providing impartial and objective advice, are so important. They are in a position to help prevent politicians from succumbing to the perennial temptations of power. Lord Butler, who was cabinet secretary and head of the home civil service between 1988 and 1998, was unquestionably right when he insisted:

> The existence of people who are not beholden to ministers for their jobs – ie, non-political civil servants – has lent a great deal to the integrity of British public life... It has been an important part of keeping our government straight.[1]

It has also had an important role in improving policy. It is very easy for politicians, especially ones flushed with electoral success, to deceive themselves about the merits of their own policies, and to believe that, finally, they have found the answers to the problems that their predecessors in office tried but failed to solve. Objective and impartial scrutiny of those policies can prevent policy blunders and it can improve flawed proposals. So can the awareness of what happened last time. Very few political ideas are wholly new. Most of them have been tried at some point in the past. Permanent officials can provide what can be a critically important reminder of what experience has demonstrated will be the likely effects of implementing a particular policy. To the extent that they are not doing this at present – and I have explained some of the reasons why they are not – it is a serious impediment to good government.

In a democracy, democratically-elected politicians must always have the last word. The importance of impartial and objective officials who are committed to honesty and integrity is not that they should be able to stop politicians from doing what they have been elected to do, but that officials should be able to improve politicians' policies, and to make it more likely those policies comply with the requirements of legality and constitutional propriety. This is not a role which the politically committed can be expected to fulfil with anything like the same degree of competence. The Public Administration Select Committee reports Francis Maude as saying: 'You are much more likely to get candid and often brutal advice from your special advisers who have no tenure at all except your will'.[2] But that is simply not true. You are *not* likely to get 'candid and often brutal advice' from those who share your political convictions. They will inevitably fall into the same traps of wishful thinking that you have. Francis Maude's assertion is the equivalent of thinking that the best person to provide a referee for a football game is an individual who is a committed supporter of one of the two competing teams.

Granting any individual, group or institution completely unconstrained political power is always dangerous: it always carries the risk that those who have unconstrained power will abuse it. The people are sovereign – but within limits, because we the people recognise that not everything the people vote for should be done immediately, or even at all. Just as the law requires that most big purchases now come with a mandatory cooling off period, where the individual can think about whether or not he really wants to spend all that money on a time-share in Spain, so the policies that have been 'bought' by a majority of the electorate need to be assessed by people who do not already believe that they are the right thing to do. That is the function of an independent civil service: in providing impartial and objective advice, it increases the chances that policies that will later be regretted are not implemented in haste.

The increasing prevalence of special advisers has coincided with the arrival of new governments made up of politicians who lack ministerial experience. Since Margaret Thatcher's election victory in 1979, the pattern has been for the losing party to spend many years in opposition before regaining power. When Labour finally won a general election under Tony Blair, in 1997, not a single member of his cabinet had ever previously held cabinet rank. When, 13 years later, Labour was replaced by the Conservative-Liberal Democrat coalition led by David Cameron, only two cabinet ministers – William Hague and Kenneth Clarke – had any experience of being in the cabinet. That contrasts strikingly with the ministers sitting around Mrs Thatcher's cabinet table in 1979, eight of whom (including the prime minister herself) had been in the cabinet before, or those around the cabinet table when Labour won in 1974, nine of whom had been in the cabinet before, or again with the cabinet Edward Heath put together after he won in 1970, in which eight members had already held cabinet office.

The lack of ministerial experience amongst the members of newly-elected governments means they badly need the advice of civil servants who understand the administrative machine and what it can, and what it cannot, do. At the same time, newly appointed ministers with no experience of government are least likely to take the advice of civil servants. Long periods in opposition have the effect of heightening a new minister's suspicion of officials: there is a sense that they have been 'captured' by the other side, and cannot be trusted. Being out of office usually reinforces the inexperienced incoming minster's conviction that compromising ideological commitments in order to achieve practical and effective policies amounts to a defeatist acceptance of the status quo – which is precisely what new ministers feel they have been elected to change. As a consequence, they tend to believe that nothing is to be learned from the experience of civil servants. It is one of the principal reasons why recent governments have looked to special advisers, rather than experienced officials, for advice on policy. That outlook does not reverse itself. Once they have been in office for a few years, ministers who arrived thinking that they needed special advisers in order to get around what they originally perceived to be recalcitrant officials do not come to the view that they can diminish the role of their advisers. Special advisers do not diminish over time. They only increase.

There are many things wrong with the civil service as it now is, and many things that can be done to improve it. But our government would not improve if its role in providing objective and impartial assessment of policy was totally supplanted by politically committed special advisers. If present trends continue, however, that is what will eventually happen. What can be done to stop the movement towards that destination, or at least to slow it down? Anyone who wishes to diminish the role played by special advisers faces the following problem: it is ministers who have increased the power and number of special advisers, and it is ministers alone who can reduce it. But they think they have no interest at all in doing so. On the contrary, the increasing emphasis in contemporary democratic politics on presentation and publicity means that ministers, and especially the prime minister, place ever-greater emphasis on the sort of expertise that special advisers, as opposed to civil servants, provide: the ability to anticipate the political effects of making an announcement, rather than the assessment of the long-term consequences for the country of adopting a particular policy. This is not an attitude that varies across members of different political parties. All of them, once in office, appear to view the relative merits of special advisers and civil servants in the same way.

Special advisers are not required to have any training for their role - which is not surprising, because there is none. Most of them do not have any experience of government or administration prior to taking their first job as an adviser either. Their appointment is entirely in the gift of the secretary of state of the relevant department: the only fetter on the secretary of state's discretion is the need to secure the agreement of the prime minister. The most effective way – indeed it may be the only way – to diminish the dangers of replacing the impartial scrutiny of policy by purely political advice would be to make special advisers more like civil servants: to change the way they are appointed, so that there was some form of merit test involved, and to require that advisers, either as candidates for the job or prior to starting it, undergo compulsory training on the importance of honesty and integrity in government service, and perhaps on the nature of administrative law. It would not be a substitute for imbibing the civil service ethos, with its traditions of impartiality, integrity, objectivity and honesty. But it would be a start.

It would, however, diminish a minister's discretion on who was appointed, a move that would be strongly resisted. According to a longstanding convention, ministers are responsible for anything done by members of their department, and are answerable to parliament for it. Increasingly, ministers regard this doctrine of extensive ministerial responsibility as unfair – and particularly so if they cannot choose their senior staff, the people who will inevitably in fact make most of the decisions on how a given policy is implemented or (to use the current jargon) 'delivered'.

The convention that the act of any civil servant in their department is ultimately the act of the minister in charge, is resented and is being eroded. Ministers do not now resign if one of their civil servants is found to have done something that they feel they have to apologise to parliament for. Senior civil servants, rather than the minister, are now frequently hauled up in front of select committees in order to be held to account for what has gone wrong with the implementation of a particular policy. Ministers would like to be able to make a sharp distinction between policy and implementation, so that they are held responsible for the success of a policy, but not for the blunders of its implementation.

In reality, this distinction can rarely be made clearly or cleanly: identifying whether what went wrong was the fault of the policy or the way it was implemented frequently depends on whether you think the policy was a sensible one to adopt in the first place. The answer you give to that question almost always depends on your political convictions.[3] That is why being able to choose their own political advisers is so important to ministers, and why they have exerted increasing pressure to try to ensure that they can choose their own permanent secretaries as well.[4]

There is a further difficulty with any proposal that aims to make special advisers more like civil servants: as far as ministers are concerned, the whole point of special advisers is that they are *not* like civil servants. They do not think like them, and they do not act like them. The more special advisers become like civil servants – the more they are concerned, not with party political considerations, and with advancing party political projects, but with the provision of objective and impartial advice, with telling the truth about the likely effects of the implementation of a particular policy – the less use they are to ministers. This is why the dispute between the respective roles of the civil service and special advisers is not a cosmetic issue, but a fundamental conflict, and one on which, in the end, compromise is more or less impossible – just as it was between Northcote's and Trevelyan's vision of what the executive arm of government should be like, and the system of unmeritocratic, politicised jobbery that their report aimed to overthrow.

It should not be impossible to convince our political representatives that it is in their, as well as our, interests to increase the role of the objective and impartial advice in the formation and implementation of policy. Northcote and Trevelyan and their supporters managed to secure enough supporters to defeat the old system, although it took more than 50 years to implement their report fully. The trouble is, we the people just don't seem very concerned about the matter, which leaves the politicians free to erode the role of the civil service in providing impartial advice. It is important that a way is found to make the electorate aware of how important matters of procedure are: failing to get them right will diminish the quality of government, and therefore the quality of life, in our country. And we need to do it quickly, before the process of dismantling the civil service as Northcote, Trevelyan and their successors conceived it has become irreversible.

Bibliography

1. Parliamentary and government reports

'Defining the Boundaries within the Executive: Ministers, Special Advisers and the permanent Civil Service', Committee on Standards in Public Life (Wicks Committee), 2003. Oral and written evidence.

Report of the Joint Committee on the Draft Constitutional Renewal Bill, Volume II, 2008.

Committee on Public Administration, Session 2003-2003: minutes of evidence.

The Leveson Inquiry: Culture, Practices and Ethics of the Press, 2012. Report and evidence.

House of Lords Debates, Hansard.

'Special Advisers: Boon or Bane?', House of Commons Public Administration Select Committee, 2001.

'These Unfortunate Events', House of Commons Public Administration Select Committee, 2002.

'Special advisers in the thick of it', House of Commons Public Administration Select Committee, 2012.

'Truth to power: how Civil Service reform can succeed', House of Commons Public Administration Select Committee, 2013.

'The accountability of civil servants', House of Lords Constitution Committee, 2012.

2. Books and articles

Acemoglu, Daron, and Robinson, James A., *Why Nations Fail: The Origins of Power, Prosperity and Poverty*, London: Profile, 2013.

Barber, Michael, *Instruction to Deliver: Fighting to Transform Britain's Public Services*, London: Methuen, 2008.

Blair, Tony, speech on modernisation of the civil service, 24 February 2004.

Blick, Andrew, *People Who Live in the Dark*, London: Politico's, 2004.

Crewe, Ivor, 'Fit-for-purpose Whitehall', Reform, 2014.

Cummings, Dominic, 'The hollow men II: Some reflections on Westminster and Whitehall dysfunction', Dominic Cummings's Blog, 30 October 2014 .

Cusick, James, 'Dump f***ing everyone: The inside story of how Michael Gove's vicious attack dogs are terrorising the DfE', *The Independent*, 15 February 2013.

Diamond, Patrick, 'Governing as New Labour: An Inside Account of the Blair and Brown Years', *Political Studies Review* (Vol 9, Issue 2), 8 April 2011.

Harris, Josh, 'One direction: first accounting officer ministerial direction published since 2010', Institute for Government, 2015.

Hennessy, Peter, *Whitehall*, London: Martin Secker & Warburg, 1989.

Heywood, Jeremy, and Kerslake, Bob, 'Tribute to Baroness Thatcher', *The Daily Telegraph*, 15 April 2013.

Hillman, Nick, *In Defence of Special Advisers: Lessons from Personal Experience*, Institute for Government, 2014.

King, Anthony, and Crewe, Ivor, *The Blunders of Our Governments*, London: Oneworld, 2013.

Lankester, Tim, *The Politics and Economics of Britain's Foreign Aid: The Pergau Dam Affair*, London: Routledge, 2013.

Letwin, Oliver, 'Why mandarins matter', Institute for Government, 2012.

Maude, Francis, 'Ministers and mandarins: Speaking truth unto power', Policy Exchange, 5 June 2013.

Miller, Joel, 'Profiling Populations Available for Stops and Searches', Home Office, Police Research Series Paper 131, 2000.

Miller, Joel, Quinton, P., and Bland, N., 'Police stops and searches: lessons from a programme of research', Home Office, Briefing Note, 2000.

Miller, Joel, Bland, N., and Quinton, P., 'The Impact of Stops and Searches on Crime and the Community', Home Office, Police Research Series Paper 127, 2000.

Mountfield, Robin, '"Politicisation" and the Civil Service: A note', *Civil Servant*, 2002.

Powell, Jonathan, *The New Machiavelli: How to Wield Power in the Modern World*, London: Vintage, 2011.

Quinton, P., Bland, N., and Miller, J., 'Police Stops, Decision-making and Practice', Home Office, Police Research Series Paper 130, 2000.

'Shriti Vadera: A profile of the Business Minister nicknamed "Shriti the Shriek"', *The Daily Telegraph*, 15 January 2009.

Sisson, C.H., *The Spirit of British Administration and Some European Comparisons*, London: Faber & Faber, 1959.

Slack, Becky, 'A sense of direction', *Civil Service World*, 28 March 2012.

Stratton, Allegra, 'Francis Maude attacks Civil Service over job document', BBC News, 7 July 2014.

Sumption, Jonathan, 'Judicial and political decision-making: The uncertain boundary', F.A. Mann Lecture, Lincoln's Inn, 2011.

Terzi, Alessio, 'Corruptionomics in Italy: Why and how fighting corruption matters for economic growth', Breugel, 22 May 2015.

Waddington, P. A. J., Stenson, K., and Don, D., 'In proportion: race, and police stop and search', *British Journal of Criminology* 44 (pp.889-914), 2004.

Wilkes, Giles, 'The Unelected Lynchpin: Why Government Needs Special Advisers', Institute for Government, 2014.

Williams, Bernard, *Moral Luck*, Cambridge: Cambridge University Press, 1981.

Wilson, Harold, *The Governance of Britain*, London: Weidenfeld & Nicholson, 1976.

Wittgenstein, Ludwig, *Philosophical Investigations*, trans. G.E.M. Anscombe: Oxford: Blackwell, 1976.

Yong, Ben, and Hazell, Robert, *Special Advisers: Who they are, what they do, and why they matter*, Oxford: Hart, 2014.

Notes

Introduction: No Sir Humphrey

1   Acemoglu and Robinson, in *Why Nations Fail: the Origins of Power, Prosperity and Poverty*, provide a persuasive survey.

2   The phrase is Oliver Letwin's. See his extremely clear and mostly persuasive speech to the Institute of Government, 'Why Mandarins Matter'. Letwin is Conservative MP for West Dorset. He was appointed chancellor of the Duchy of Lancaster in 2014. He has overall responsibility for the Cabinet Office, and advises the prime minister on the implementation of government policy.

3   I was alerted to this by Lord Saatchi's speech to the Lords, 1 May 2002.

4   'The accountability of civil servants', House of Lords Constitution Committee, Evidence, p.135.

5   For an idea of the appalling effects of a corrupt bureaucracy in a developed European economy, see Alessio Terzi on Italy: 'Corruptionomics in Italy: Why and How Fighting Corruption Matters for Economic Growth'. He quotes a statistic from the Italian Court of Auditors, which estimates that for large public works, corruption amounts to as much as 40 per cent of total public procurement value.

1. Impartiality, objectivity, honesty and integrity

1   Yong and Hazell, in *Special Advisers: Who they are, what they do, and why they matter*, provide many quotations from ministers and others to support their assertion that 'special advisers have become an established part of British government: ministers cannot now imagine doing without them'.

2   Clarke, Charles, evidence to Committee on Standards in Public Life, 9 July 2002, paragraph 2383.

3   Maude, 'Ministers and mandarins: Speaking truth unto power'.

4   Letwin, 'Why mandarins matter'. He did not give any examples of civil servants successfully delaying, and thereby defeating, the implementation of an elected government's policies. Although Letwin's assertion is one of those claims that is generally accepted

by politicians, it is in fact quite hard to come up with concrete cases of successful civil service obstruction. Michael Barber, who was appointed by Tony Blair to oversee the implementation of New Labour's policies, first in the Department for Education, and then across Whitehall, maintains that civil servants at the Department for Education resisted putting into practice Labour's idea that central government should have the power to intervene directly in poorly performing education authorities. Their resistance was not successful. See his *Instruction to Deliver*, p.313. It is rather easier to find instances when civil servants failed even to try to prevent ministers from implementing what turned out to be a disastrous policy: the most obvious case is the poll tax.

5   Sisson, *The Spirit of British Administration and Some European Comparisons*, p.143.

6   'Truth to power: how Civil Service reform can succeed', House of Commons Public Administration Select Committee Evidence, p.47.

7   Wilson, *The Governance of Britain*, pp.202-205.

8   Blick, A., *People Who Live in the Dark*, chapter 2, pp.30-63, provides a good account of Wilson's experiment with special advisers.

9   Wilson, *The Governance of Britain*, p.204.

10   Blick, *People Who Live in the Dark*, p.57

11   Yong and Hazell, *Special Advisers*, chapter 3, pp.35-60.

12   Evidence to the Lords Constitution Committee, 18 July 2012, response to Q357 from Lord Crickhowell.

13   Stratton, 'Francis Maude attacks Civil Service over job document'.

2. 'This is shit': The marginalisation of civil servants

1   It has been put to me that several secretaries of state instituted the practice that no advice should be put to them until their special advisers have commented on it and re-worked it so that it complies with political imperatives. I cannot find anything which formally orders or even records that practice – but that is not surprising, since it is an informal process, rather than one mandated by government policy.

2   Mountfield, '"Politicisation" and the Civil Service: A note'.

3   Evidence to the Joint Committee on the Draft Constitutional Renewal Bill, Vol II, p.201.

4   Evidence to the Joint Committee of the Houses of Parliament on the Draft Constitutional Renewal Bill, Vol II, p.193, 10 June 2008.

5   House of Commons Liaison Committee, 16 July 2002, response to Q8 from Tony Wright.

6   House of Lords Debate, 7 November 2005. Alastair Campbell had by then retired, leaving only Powell with explicitly granted executive authority.

7   Written evidence submitted to Public Administration Select Committee for report 'Special advisers in the thick of it'.

8   'Special Advisers: Boon or Bane?', Public Administration Select Committee, par 61.

9   Ibid, p.96.

10 Michael Jacobs, 'Special Advisers in the thick of it', House of Commons Public Administration, Written Evidence.

11 Paul Richards, 'The accountability of civil servants', House of Lords Constitution Committee, Oral Evidence, 20 June 2012.

12 Ibid, p.96.

13 Powell, *The New Machiavelli*, p.21.

14 'These Unfortunate Events', Public Administration Select Committee.

15 'Defining the Boundaries within the Executive: Ministers, Special Advisers and the permanent Civil Service', Committee on Standards in Public Life, p.236, pars 2762-2767. Lord Wilson's circumspection may be explained by the fact that, as he said at par 2744: 'I am here to represent the government'.

16 'Shriti Vadera's fierce reputation earned her the nickname "Shriti the Shriek"', *The Daily Telegraph*.

17 Cusick, 'Dump f***ing everyone: The inside story of how Michael Gove's vicious attack dogs are terrorising the DfE'.

18 'The accountability of civil servants', House of Lords Constitution Committee, p.65.

19 Hillman, *In Defence of Special Advisers*, pp.18-19.

20 Cummings, 'The hollow men II: Some reflections on Westminster and Whitehall dysfunction', p.9.

21 House of Lords Debates, 7 November 2005, Hansard Column 490.

22 Report of the Joint Committee on the Draft Constitutional Renewal Bill, Volume II, par 20.

23 The exchange between Richards and Powell is to be found on p.104 of 'The accountability of civil servants', House of Lords Constitution Committee.

24 Hillman, *In Defence of Special Advisers*, p16.

25 Joint Committee on the Constitutional Reform Bill, Evidence, p.207.

26 Wilkes, *The Unelected Lynchpin*.

27 Leveson Inquiry, Witness Statement of Jonathan Stephens, par 26; Jonathan Stephens oral evidence, 25 May 2012, afternoon session, page 29 lines 13 and 14.

28 Lord Hart in 'The accountability of civil servants', House of Lords Constitution Committee, Evidence, p.25; Charles Clarke's comment is on pp.64-65.

29 Sir Jeremy Heywood's letter is quoted in 'Special Advisers in the thick of it', House of Commons Public Administration Select Committee, paragraph 27. The report has a very clear summary of the reasons for Adam Smith's resignation.

30 Quoted in Yong and Hazell, *Special Advisers*, p.175.

3. The new Machiavellis and the job of the court

1 It is reprinted in Williams, *Moral Luck*.

2 Powell, *The New Machiavelli*, p.84.

3 It is striking that Powell does not make telling the truth to the public the 'first requirement' of 'a member of the court' – by which he means any official working directly to the prime minister inside Number 10. The first requirement for that role, he says, is 'loyalty and confidentiality' (*The New Machiavelli*, p.84). This may well be good advice for political effectiveness, which is Powell's concern. It does now, however, reflect the sort of priorities that we as citizens want public officials to have.

4 'A Sense of Direction', Civil Service World, and Harris, 'One direction: first accounting officer ministerial direction published since 2010'.

5 Evidence to Lords Constitution Committee, 23 May 2012, p.21.

6 Hennessy, *Whitehall*. See especially the chapter entitled 'The Thatcher Effect', which provides a good account of what happened, with references.

7 Quoted in Sir Jeremy Heywood and Sir Bob Kerslake's Tribute to Baroness Thatcher, *The Daily Telegraph*, 15 April 2013. Lord (Norman) Fowler's experience may have followed the same trajectory as Mrs Thatcher's. He told the Lords Constitution Committee that, in spite of being 'a member of the most radical government since Attlee's', he 'never at any stage found any problem with the civil service in developing, implementing and putting forward those policies… In the main, it was a Rolls-Royce machine, and I think we would be mad to turn our back on it'. Evidence to Lords Constitution Committee, 'The accountability of civil servants', p.41.

8   Diamond, 'Governing as New Labour: An Inside Account of the Blair and Brown Years', p.151; Powell, *The New Machiavelli*, p.148. The quotation on Gordon Brown comes from Crewe and King, Blunders of Our Governments, pp.259-60.

9   Blair, speech on modernisation of the civil service.

10 Lord Butler's idea that political advisers 'should no longer be classified be as civil servants' but rather 'treated like political advisers to opposition parties' would have the great merit of ending the confusion. He has made the suggestion several times since 2002. No government has seen fit to take up his proposal. See his written evidence to Public Administration Select Committee in 'Special advisers in the thick of it'.

11 King and Crewe, *Blunders of Our Governments*, p.335.

12 Lord Macdonald of Tradeston emphasised this in his evidence to the Wicks Committee, 18 September 2002, p.287, par 3323.

13 Powell, *The New Machiavelli*, p.72.

14 'Truth to power: how Civil Service reform can succeed', House of Commons Public Administration Select Committee, Evidence, Q1048, p.185.

15 'Truth to power: how Civil Service reform can succeed', House of Commons Public Administration Select Committee, Evidence, Q199, p.45.

16 'Truth to power: how Civil Service reform can succeed', House of Commons Public Administration Select Committee, Evidence, Q27, p.8.

17 Quinton, *et al*, 'Police Stops, Decision-making and Practice'; Miller *et al*, 'The Impact of Stops and Searches on Crime and the Community'; Miller *et al*, 'Profiling Populations Available for Stops and Searches'; Miller *et al*, 'Police stops and searches: lessons from a programme of research'; Waddington *et al*, 'In proportion: race, and police stop and search'.

4. The patronage virus and incompetent government

1   'The accountability of civil servants', Lords Constitution Committee, par 34.

2   The latest guidance from the Civil Service Commission on the appointment of permanent secretaries dates from December 2012. It emphasises that the prime minister has the final word on the appointment of any permanent secretary.

3   Chambers, Joshua, 'Maude set to announce move to "extended ministerial offices"', *Civil Service World*, 10 July 2013; Elliott, Francis, 'Nicky Morgan faces battles with the teaching establishment over the next round of school reforms', *The Times*, 21 July 2015.

4   'The accountability of civil servants', Lords Constitution Committee, Evidence, p.231.

5   Michael Jacobs, written evidence in 'Special Advisers in the thick of it', Public Administration Select Committee.

6   The incident is comprehensively analysed in *The Politics and Economics of Britain's Foreign Aid: The Pergau Dam Affair*, by Tim Lankester, who was the permanent secretary at the time. Lord Sumption discusses the Appeal Court's decision in 'Judicial and Political Decision-Making: The Uncertain Boundary', FA Mann Lecture, 2011.

7   Crewe, 'Fit-For-Purpose Whitehall', p.87.

8   Margaret Hodge, evidence to Lords Constitution Committee, 23 May 2012, 'The accountability of civil servants', p.13.

9   Wittgenstein, *Philosophical Investigations*, par 265, p.94.

Conclusion: Keeping our government straight

1   Evidence to Public Administration Select Committee, 19 June 2003.

2   House of Commons Public Administration Select Committee, par 21, p.27. It gives as a reference 'Ministers and Mandarins: speaking truth unto power', Maude's speech to Policy Exchange. But I cannot find the phrase in that speech. In the speech, Maude says: 'Good ministers want bright knowledgeable officials who will give the most brutally candid advice.'

3   The Lords Constitution Committee illustrates this point, and provides evidence, in 'The accountability of civil servants'.

4   It was originally part of the Conservatives' plan to reform the civil service that the appointment of a permanent secretary should be taken out of the hands of the Civil Service Commission and given to the secretary of state. There was a great deal of opposition to that idea. The compromise was that the secretary of state should have a veto on any candidate put up by the commission – although in practice, he or she already has one, and has done for many years.